BOOK OF FORMS
for Everyday Living

Louisa Rogers, Ed.D.

Educational Consultant, Florida International University
TESOL Department, Graduate School of Education

National Textbook Company
a division of NTC/CONTEMPORARY PUBLISHING GROUP
Lincolnwood, Illinois USA

Acknowledgments

Grateful acknowledgment is made to the following for permission to reprint their materials:

Barnett Bank, Jacksonville, Florida; bank credit card application

Center for Therapeutic Bodywork, Inc., patient registration/history form

The Eureka Company, product warranty and registration forms

E-Z Legal Forms, Inc., Deerfield Beach, Florida; rental/credit application

Ford Motor Credit Company, automobile loan application

Micro Warehouse, Inc., MacWarehouse® catalog cover and order form. Copyright © 1995 Micro Warehouse, Inc. All rights reserved. Reprinted with permission.

TOPS Business Forms, a subsidiary of Wallace Computer Services, Inc., job application

Design and layout: Publication Services
Cover design: Nick Panos

ISBN: 0-8442-0816-7

Published by National Textbook Company,
a division of NTC/Contemporary Publishing Group, Inc.,
4255 West Touhy Avenue,
Lincolnwood (Chicago), Illinois 60646-1975 U.S.A.
© 1997 by NTC/Contemporary Publishing Group, Inc.
Manufactured in the United States of America.
Library of Congress Catalog Card Number: 96-68780

890VL98765432

Preface

The *Book of Forms for Everyday Living* will help you learn to fill out the important forms and applications used today. Being able to fill out forms clearly and accurately will allow you to enjoy many benefits and opportunities available to everyone. You will also save time and money when you can complete forms with ease.

In this book, you will learn to master some familiar, yet complex, forms and applications. These include:

> A Social Security Application
>
> Tax Forms
>
> Checks, Deposit Tickets, and Bank Statements
>
> A Credit Card Application
>
> A Driver's License Application
>
> Voter Registration
>
> Postal Service Forms
>
> A Health History Form
>
> A Catalog Order Form
>
> An Automobile Loan Application
>
> An Employment Application

For each form, you will find new and difficult words defined and an introduction explaining the form's importance and purpose. Step-by-step instructions teach you how to fill out each form correctly.

There are plenty of opportunities to practice with actual, up-to-date forms. This practice will help you in real-life situations. The *Book of Forms for Everyday Living* will help you enjoy the many opportunities and benefits of American society.

Contents

Personal Fact Sheet 1

Unit 1 Employment Forms. 3

Application for Social Security Number 4
Application for Employment 7
Employee's Withholding Allowance Certificate, W-4 Form 10
Unemployment Compensation Application 12

Unit 2 Money Matters 17

Opening a Checking Account – A Deposit Ticket 18
A Personal Check 20
The Checkbook Register. 22
The Bank Statement 24
Federal Income Tax Form 1040EZ 25
Federal Income Tax Form 1040A. 27

Unit 3 Consumer Needs 33

Credit Card Application 34
Application for an Automobile Loan 37
Warranty Card and Registration Form 41
Catalog Order Form 43

Unit 4 Government Applications and Forms 47

Driver's License Application. 48
Parent Consent for Driver Application of Minor Under 18 50
Voter Registration. 51
Passport Application. 53
Customs Declaration 56

Unit 5 Personal Concerns 59

Marriage License Pre-Application 60
Rental/Credit Application. 62
Change of Address Order Form 66
Postal Service Postcard 68
Authorization to Hold Mail 70
Health History Form 72

Personal Fact Sheet

Before you start the practice applications and forms in this book, fill in the following personal fact sheet. It is here to help you get organized. Take a few minutes to think about the answers now. Then, when you get to the practice applications and forms, you will have much of the information already written out. You can also keep your personal fact sheet with you when you fill in real applications and forms.

If you have the fact sheet with you, you will never get stuck having to remember things like the address of your last place of employment or the telephone number of one of your references. The fact sheet is a handy record of the names, addresses, and telephone numbers you will need for many forms.

PERSONAL FACT SHEET

1. My name is (Use the full name given to you at your birth.)

    _____

    NOTE: If you are married or have legally changed your name, give your new name. If you are a married woman, your last name at birth is your **Maiden Name**.

2. I was born (Give month, day, year.) _____

3. I am now _____ years old.

4. I live at (Give full address, apartment number, city, state, county, and ZIP code. If you do not have a permanent address, you can use a PO box as your address.)

    Street address and apartment number or PO box

    _____

    City or County, State, and ZIP code

    _____

5. My telephone number is (Give area code and number.) _____
    NOTE: If you do not have a telephone, give a number where a message can be left for you.

6. My Social Security number is _____
    NOTE: If you do not have a Social Security number yet, do not worry. The first practice form in this book is a Social Security form. After you have received your Social Security number, you can come back to the personal fact sheet and fill in the number.

PERSONAL FACT SHEET (Continued)

7. I was born in (Give city and state. If you were not born in the United States, give city and country.)

    _____

8. My father's full name is _____

9. My mother's full name is (Give her name before she was married—her maiden name.)

    _____

10. Education

	Name of School	Location	Dates Attended From	To	Graduated
Grade	_____	_____	_____	_____	_____
Secondary	_____	_____	_____	_____	_____
Trade	_____	_____	_____	_____	_____
College	_____	_____	_____	_____	_____

11. In high school I studied _____

    In trade school or special school I studied _____

12. I have worked for these companies. (List all the jobs you have had. List your last job first.)

Name and Address of Company	Telephone	Dates From	To	Duties
_____	_____	_____	_____	_____
_____	_____	_____	_____	_____
_____	_____	_____	_____	_____

    NOTE: If you need more space, use a separate piece of paper.

13. My special skills are (List your special skills such as data entry, carpentry, sales, word processing, or auto mechanic.)

    _____

    _____

    NOTE: If you need more space, use a separate piece of paper.

14. References (List the names of people other than family members who know you and can recommend you to employers.)

Name	Address	Telephone	Occupation
_____	_____	_____	_____
_____	_____	_____	_____
_____	_____	_____	_____

    NOTE: If you need more space, use a separate piece of paper.

Unit 1 Employment Forms

Having a job and earning money is very important to all of us. Unit 1 of this book is about applications and forms you need as a worker.

The **Social Security Application** comes first in this unit because you cannot work without a Social Security number. Also, almost every other application or form asks for your Social Security number.

Unit 1 also has an **Employment Application**. Knowing how to fill in this form properly can help you get a job. The way you fill in a job application can show an employer that you do careful, accurate work.

After you have a job, you will fill in a **Withholding Allowance Certificate** or **W-4** form. This form tells your employer how much income tax to deduct from your paycheck. You will learn how to fill in this form in Unit 1.

If you lose your job for some reason, you may want to apply for unemployment benefits. The

Unemployment Compensation Application in Unit 1 will help you practice filling in this form.

Remember, always read an application or form all the way through before you start filling it in. Then, when you do start writing, use a blue or black pen. Never use a pencil. And, always PRINT. After you have finished filling in the application or form, read what you have written and correct any mistakes.

SOCIAL SECURITY ADMINISTRATION
Application for a Social Security Card

INSTRUCTIONS

- Please read "How To Complete This Form" on page 2.
- Print or type using black or blue ink. DO NOT USE PENC
- After you complete this form, take or mail it along with th to your nearest Social Security office.
- If you are completing this form for someone else, answer t apply to that person. Then, sign your name in question 16

1 NAME
To Be Shown On Card

FIRST   FULL MIDDLE NAME

FULL NAME AT BIRTH
IF OTHER THAN ABOVE   FIRST   FULL MIDDLE NAME

OTHER NAMES USED

2 MAILING ADDRESS
Do Not Abbreviate

STREET ADDRESS, APT. NO., PO BOX, RURAL ROUTE NO.

CITY   STATE

3 CITIZENSHIP
(Check One)

☐ U.S. Citizen ☐ Legal Alien Allowed To Work ☐ Legal Alien Not Allowed To Work ☐ Foreign Student Allowed Restricted Employment

4 SEX

☐ Male ☐ Female

5 RACE/ETHNIC DESCRIPTION
(Check One Only—Voluntary)

☐ Asian, Asian-American Or Pacific Islander ☐ Hispanic ☐ Black (Not Hispanic)

6 DATE OF BIRTH   MONTH DAY YEAR

7 PLACE OF BIRTH
(Do Not Abbreviate)   CITY   STAT

8 MOTHER'S MAIDEN NAME   FIRST   FULL MIDDLE NAME

9 FATHER'S NAME   FIRST   FULL MIDDLE NAM

in item 1 ever received a Social Security umber

to question 14.)

3

Application for Social Security Number

New Words

alien   someone who was born in another country and is not a citizen of the United States

deliberately   on purpose

ethnic   relating to a group of people who share a common culture, religion, or language

race   a group of people who share certain physical features such as skin color or eye shape

voluntary   done by choice

Introduction

In order to work in the United States, each person must have a Social Security number. The Social Security number is printed on your Social Security card. This number is yours for life, and no two people have exactly the same number. The individual number is your identification.

Employers take a certain amount of money out of each paycheck. The money is a tax and is sent to the United States government. For as long as you work, you will pay Social Security taxes. Then, when you retire or cannot work any more, the government will make Social Security payments to you.

Even if you are not working now, you need a Social Security card because many other forms ask for your Social Security number.

The card is easy to get. Just go a Social Security office near you and fill out an application. If you are a United States citizen, bring a birth certificate and either a driver's license or passport. If you are not a United States citizen, you must show your birth certificate or passport and the documents given to you by the Immigration and Naturalization Service (INS).

NOTE: You must bring the original documents or a certified copy. Uncertified photocopies are not accepted.

After a few weeks, your Social Security card will be mailed to you.

Directions

Number 1: Number 1 on the application has three different lines for information about your name. Be sure you complete only the line(s) that you should. On line 1, print your full name, first name first.

Write on line 2 only if you have changed your name. If the name you gave on line 1 is different from the name you were given at birth, fill in your full name at birth here.

Line 3 is only for people who have changed their name more than once. If you have used a name other than the ones on the first and second lines, put that name on line 3.

NOTE: Do not use nicknames on line 1, 2, or 3.

Number 2: Fill in your full address. Make sure it is correct because your Social Security card will be mailed to the address you give.

Number 3: Put a (✓) in the box which describes you. If you are a United States citizen, put a (✓) in the box that says *U.S. citizen.*

Number 4: Put a (✓) in the appropriate box.

Number 5: You do not have to answer Number 5 in order to get a Social Security card, but it helps the government to have this information. In most cases, it is against the law to ask a person's race. However, the government keeps records which do not have the names of individuals. If you wish to answer Number 5, put a (✓) in the box that describes you.

Directions continue on page 6.

SOCIAL SECURITY ADMINISTRATION
Application for a Social Security Card

Form Approved
OMB No. 0960-0066

INSTRUCTIONS	• Please read "How To Complete This Form" on page 2.
	• Print or type using black or blue ink. DO NOT USE PENCIL.
	• After you complete this form, take or mail it along with the required documents to your nearest Social Security office.
	• If you are completing this form for someone else, answer the questions as they apply to that person. Then, sign your name in question 16.

1 NAME
To Be Shown On Card

▶ FIRST ___ FULL MIDDLE NAME ___ LAST ___

FULL NAME AT BIRTH
IF OTHER THAN ABOVE

FIRST ___ FULL MIDDLE NAME ___ LAST ___

OTHER NAMES USED ___

2 MAILING ADDRESS
Do Not Abbreviate

▶ STREET ADDRESS, APT. NO., PO BOX, RURAL ROUTE NO.

CITY ___ STATE ___ ZIP CODE ___

3 CITIZENSHIP
(Check One)

☐ U.S. Citizen   ☐ Legal Alien Allowed To Work   ☐ Legal Alien Not Allowed To Work   ☐ Foreign Student Allowed Restricted Employment   ☐ Conditionally Legalized Alien Allowed To Work   ☐ Other (See Instructions On Page 2)

4 SEX

☐ Male   ☐ Female

5 RACE/ETHNIC DESCRIPTION
(Check One Only—Voluntary)

☐ Asian, Asian-American Or Pacific Islander   ☐ Hispanic   ☐ Black (Not Hispanic)   ☐ North American Indian Or Alaskan Native   ☐ White (Not Hispanic)

☐ Office Use Only

6 DATE OF BIRTH ___
MONTH DAY YEAR

7 PLACE OF BIRTH ___
(Do Not Abbreviate)   CITY   STATE OR FOREIGN COUNTRY   FCI

8 MOTHER'S MAIDEN NAME

FIRST ___ FULL MIDDLE NAME ___ LAST NAME AT HER BIRTH ___

9 FATHER'S NAME   FIRST ___ FULL MIDDLE NAME ___ LAST ___

10 Has the person in item 1 ever received a Social Security number before?

☐ Yes (If "yes", answer questions 11-13.)   ☐ No (If "no", go on to question 14.)   ☐ Don't Know (If "don't know", go on to question 14.)

11 Enter the Social Security number previously assigned to the person listed in item 1.

☐☐☐ – ☐☐ – ☐☐☐☐

12 Enter the name shown on the most recent Social Security card issued for the person listed in item 1.

FIRST ___ MIDDLE ___ LAST ___

13 Enter any different date of birth if used on an earlier application for a card. ___
MONTH DAY YEAR

14 TODAY'S DATE ▶ ___
MONTH DAY YEAR

15 DAYTIME PHONE NUMBER ▶ (___)
AREA CODE

DELIBERATELY FURNISHING (OR CAUSING TO BE FURNISHED) FALSE INFORMATION ON THIS APPLICATION IS A CRIME PUNISHABLE BY FINE OR IMPRISONMENT, OR BOTH.

16 YOUR SIGNATURE

▶ ___

17 YOUR RELATIONSHIP TO THE PERSON IN ITEM 1 IS:

☐ Self   ☐ Natural Or Adoptive Parent   ☐ Legal Guardian   ☐ Other (Specify)

DO NOT WRITE BELOW THIS LINE (FOR SSA USE ONLY)				
NPN	DOC	NTI	CAN	ITV
PBC	EVI	EVA	EVC	PRA	NWR	DNR	UNIT

EVIDENCE SUBMITTED

SIGNATURE AND TITLE OF EMPLOYEE(S) REVIEWING EVIDENCE AND/OR CONDUCTING INTERVIEW

DATE

DCL ___ DATE

Form **SS-5** (9/89) 5/88 edition may be used until supply is exhausted

5

Number 6: Fill in your date of birth—month, day, and year.

Number 7: Fill in your place of birth, city and state. If you were not born in the United States, fill in the name of the country where you were born.

Number 8: Fill in your mother's full name, first name first, then middle name, then her *maiden name* or last name at her birth.

Number 9: Fill in your father's full name, first name first, then middle name, then last name.

Number 10: Have you ever had a Social Security number before? If you have, you must put a (✓) in the box that says *yes*. If you answer *yes* to Number 10, you must answer Numbers 11 through 13. If you have **not** had a Social Security number before, put a (✓) in the box that says *no*. If you answer *no* to Number 10, you can go directly to Number 14. If you do not know if you had a Social Security number before, put a (✓) in the box that says *don't know*, and go directly to Number 14.

Number 11: DO THIS ONLY IF YOU ANSWERED YES TO NUMBER 10. Fill in the Social Security number you had before.

Number 12: DO THIS ONLY IF YOU ANSWERED YES TO NUMBER 10. Fill in your name as it appeared on the Social Security card you had before.

Number 13: DO THIS ONLY IF YOU ANSWERED YES TO NUMBER 10. If you used a different date of birth on an earlier application, fill in that date of birth here.

Number 14: Fill in the date. You can use today's date on the practice application. When you fill in the **REAL** application, use the date at that time.

Number 15: Fill in your phone number or a phone number where a message can be left for you. Put your area code first.

Number 16: Sign your name. DO NOT PRINT.

Number 17: If you are filling in the application for yourself, put a (✓) in the box that says *self*. If you are filling in the application for someone else, put a (✓) in the box that describes your relationship to that person.

NOTE: Do not fill in anything after Number 17.

Application for Employment

New Words

Age Discrimination in Employment Act a federal law forbidding employers to refuse to hire workers who are at least 40 but under 70 years old

bona fide real; true

discrimination treating people differently because of race, sex, age, or national origin

enlistment joining (usually the military)

limitation something that would stop you from performing a job or task

occupation job

permissible allowed

preceding coming before

prohibit keep from; not allow

qualifications skills; what you can do

questionnaire a form that asks questions which need to be answered

reference a person who knows something about your personality and/or skills

Introduction

Your new Social Security card has come in the mail. Now you can look for a job. Remember, you cannot work until you get a Social Security number.

When you apply for a job, the first step is to fill in the application for employment. Be very careful when filling in this form. If you make many mistakes, the person who reads your application will think that you did not take the time to read and follow the instructions. If you cannot follow the instructions for filling in an application, what kind of worker will you be?

After you fill in the application for employment, someone from the personnel office will interview you.

Special Tip: Looking for a job or "job hunting" is difficult for many people. You can begin by looking in the classified ad section of your local newspaper. You can also go to a private employment agency for help. Private employment agencies charge money for their help. Sometimes you pay the fee. Sometimes the employer pays the fee. Find out who pays the fee before letting an agency help you. There are also state employment agencies. Their help is free.

NOTE: This application says "An Equal Opportunity Employer." This means the employer offers equal chances for employment to all people who apply, no matter what their race, sex, or age.

NOTE: Not all employment application forms look exactly like this one, but they all have similar questions.

Directions

Top Section
At the top right side of the application is a line for the date. Do not forget to fill in the date.

Number 1: Print your full name. On this application, put your last name then your first name. To the right, fill in your Social Security number.

Number 2: Fill in your full address. Then, fill in your telephone number. **NOTE:** This form does not ask for your area code, but you should include it before your telephone number.

Number 3: Fill in the kind of job you are applying for (for example—mail clerk, mechanic, or receptionist).

Directions continue on page 9.

APPLICATION FOR EMPLOYMENT

(PRE-EMPLOYMENT QUESTIONNAIRE)   (AN EQUAL OPPORTUNITY EMPLOYER)

Date _____

1. Name [Last Name First] _____ Soc. Sec. No. _____

2. Address _____ Telephone _____

3. What kind of work are you applying for? _____

4. What special qualifications do you have? _____

5. What office machines can you operate? _____

6. Are you 18 years or older? Yes _____ No _____

SPECIAL PURPOSE QUESTIONS

DO NOT ANSWER **ANY** OF THE QUESTIONS IN THIS FRAMED AREA UNLESS THE EMPLOYER HAS **CHECKED A BOX PRECEDING** A QUESTION, THEREBY INDICATING THAT THE INFORMATION IS REQUIRED FOR A BONA FIDE OCCUPATIONAL QUALIFICATION, OR DICTATED BY NATIONAL SECURITY LAWS, OR IS NEEDED FOR OTHER LEGALLY PERMISSIBLE REASONS.

☐ HEIGHT _____ FEET _____ INCHES _____ ☐ WEIGHT _____ LBS. ☐ CITIZEN OF U.S. YES _____ NO _____

☐ _____

_____

MILITARY SERVICE RECORD

1. Armed Forces Service _____ Yes _____ No _____ From* _____ To* _____

2. Branch of Service _____ Duties _____

3. Rank or rating at time of enlistment _____ Rating at time of discharge _____

4. Do you have any physical limitations that prohibit you from performing any work for which you are being considered? Yes _____ No _____. Please describe. _____

_____

EDUCATION

SCHOOL	*NO. OF YEARS ATTENDED	NAME OF SCHOOL	CITY	COURSE	*DID YOU GRADUATE?
GRAMMAR					
HIGH					
COLLEGE					
OTHER					

*The Age Discrimination in Employment Act of 1967 prohibits discrimination on the basis of age with respect to individuals who are at least 40 but less than 70 years of age.

EXPERIENCE

NAME AND ADDRESS OF COMPANY	DATE FROM	DATE TO	LIST YOUR DUTIES	STARTING SALARY	FINAL SALARY	REASON FOR LEAVING

BUSINESS REFERENCES

NAME	ADDRESS	OCCUPATION

This form has been designed to strictly comply with State and Federal fair employment practice laws prohibiting employment discrimination. This Application for Employment Form is sold for general use throughout the United States. TOPS assumes no responsibility for the inclusion in said form of any questions which, when asked by the Employer of the Job Applicant, may violate State and/or Federal Law.

TOPS 🔹 Form 3286 (Revised)

Litho in U.S.A.

Number 4: Give the special skills or qualifications you have for this job. For example, if you are applying for a job as a sales person, your qualifications might be that you can speak three different languages.

Number 5: List the office machines you know how to use (for example—fax machine, computer, copy machine).

Number 6: Put a (✓) next to the *yes* or *no.*

Special Purpose Questions Section

Do not fill in this section unless the employer has put a check (✓) next to some or all of the boxes. The employer cannot ask you these questions unless the job you are applying for requires you to be a certain height and weight. Some government jobs require you to be a U.S. citizen. Also, some forms ask for information about criminal records. This information can only be requested if you are applying for a job such as that of a security guard.

Military Service Record Section

Number 1: If you were in the armed forces or military, put a (✓) next to *yes.* Then, give the dates you were in the armed forces. If you were not in the armed forces, put a (✓) next to *no,* and skip the rest of this section.

Number 2: Give the name of the branch of the armed forces you were in (for example—Army, Navy, Air Force, Marines, or Coast Guard). Then, list your duties.

Number 3: Give your rank when you enlisted. Then, give your rank when you were discharged.

Number 4: If you do **not** have any physical limitations, put a (✓) next to *no.* If you do have physical limitations, put a (✓) next to *yes,* and explain what you cannot do.

Education Section

Fill in the number of years you went to each school. Then, fill in the name of the school and the city it is in. Where it says *course,* fill in what you studied. Most of the time you can write *general* or *academic.* Then, answer *yes* or *no* in the space *Did you Graduate?* The line *Other* is for any special training you have or special trade school you went to (for example—a computer programming course).

Experience Section

Give the name and address of each company you worked for. Start with your most recent job on the first line. If you are still working at that job, it is o.k. to list it. Then, fill in the dates you worked for each company. Next list your duties—what you did. Write how much you were paid—your salary, when you started the job, and how much you were paid when you left. You may write this number as an hourly salary or a weekly salary (for example—$8.00 per hr, or $320.00 per wk). Finally, give the reason you left that job. If you are still working at that job, give the reason you are planning to leave. You can say you want a higher salary or more job responsibility.

Business References Section

Your business references are people you have worked for. They were pleased with you as a worker.

Tip: It is always a good idea to ask people if you can use their name as a reference. That way you can be sure they will say good things about you. Give the names and addresses of people who you are sure will give you good references. Also, give their occupation.

Read through your application to make sure everything is correct.

Good luck with your interview.

Employee's Withholding Allowance Certificate, W-4 Form

New Words

allowance the number of people you support, including yourself. These people are your dependents; they depend on you.

deduct subtract

exempt free from, not responsible for

penalty a punishment for breaking the law

perjury lying when you have sworn to tell the truth

refund something you get back

withhold keep back

Introduction

Congratulations! Your application for employment was filled in correctly, and your interview went well. You got the job. Now you must complete the Employee's Withholding Allowance Certificate, known as the W-4 form.

The government of the United States requires everyone who works to pay a tax. This is called income tax because it is a tax on what you earn—your income. When you get your paycheck, income tax will have been taken out and sent to the government.

This is different from Social Security tax which you learned about at the beginning of this unit. Your income tax money pays for government services and operations. For example, your congressperson and senator are paid salaries for the jobs they do. Your income tax money pays their salaries.

The amount of income tax you pay depends on two things The first is how much money you make. In the United States, the more money you make, the more income tax you pay. The second is how many allowances or dependents you have. You get one allowance for yourself. If you support other people (for example—children), you can have more allowances. The people you support are called dependents. There is one allowance for each dependent. The more allowances you have, the less income tax is deducted from your paycheck.

When you fill in the W-4 form, you let your employer know how many allowances you have, so the correct amount of income tax can be deducted from your paycheck.

Directions

Number 1: Print your full name. On this form, your first name goes first. Do not forget to print your middle initial. The two lines below your name are for your address.

Number 2: Fill in your Social Security number.

Number 3: Put a (✓) in the appropriate box.

Number 4: If the last name you have on your Social Security card is different from the name you used on your W-4, call the "800" number written on this form. Also, put a check (✓) in the box at the right.

Number 5: Fill in the number of allowances you have. For example, if your two children and your mother live with you and you support them, you have four (4) allowances—two allowances for your children, one for your mother, and one for yourself.

Number 6: Do **not** fill in this part unless you want more money withheld from your paycheck. If you do, fill in how much more.

Number 7: If you did not owe any income tax last year and think you will not owe any this year, write the word *exempt* here. If you do claim tax exemption, you must be sure that you are not claimed as an allowance or dependent on someone else's tax form.

Sign the W-4 form where it says *Employee's signature* at the bottom. Also, make sure you fill in the date. Your employer will fill in Numbers 8 through 10.

Unemployment Compensation Application

New Words

benefit   a payment; bonus or advantage

compensation   something that makes up for something else

impairment   disability; handicap; damage

confidential   something secret or private

discharge   fire; lay off

gross income/earnings   income before taxes are deducted

in lieu of   in place of

misconduct   wrong or bad behavior

severance pay   money you may receive from your employer when you are discharged

retirement pension   money you receive after you stop working at a certain age. This is money that both you and your employer have saved for years.

wages   salary; money earned

felony   a very serious crime

misdemeanor   a less serious crime; misbehavior

Introduction

What happens if your employer does not need you any more or cannot pay you any more? Everyone hopes this will not happen, but sometimes it does. If you lose your job, you can apply for unemployment compensation.

While you are employed, your employer pays money to the government. If you are discharged, you can receive money—unemployment compensation—from the government while you look for another job.

You can receive unemployment compensation every week for a maximum of 26 weeks. During this time, you must prove you are looking for a job. The amount of money you get depends on what you earned during the 12 months before you were discharged.

NOTE: Unemployment compensation is **not** for people who are fired for misconduct or who quit for personal reasons. Unemployment compensation is for people who are discharged even though they are good workers.

Directions

NOTE: Make sure you PRINT.

Number 1: Fill in your full name, first name first.

Number 1a: If you used a different name at work, fill that name in here.

Number 2: Fill in your complete address.

Number 3: Fill in you telephone number, area code first. If you have a second telephone number, put that in the space that says *alternate*.

Number 4: Fill in your date of birth.

Number 5: Put a (✓) in the correct box.

Number 6: Fill in your height in feet and inches and your weight in pounds.

Number 7: Put a (✓) in the box that describes your ethnic group. **NOTE:** The government uses this for information only. The government does **not** consider your ethnic group when paying unemployment compensation.

Directions continue on page 15.

NOTICE: Information you provide to this agency is confidential. However, the Federal Deficit Reduction Act, an amendment to the Federal Social Security Act, provides that upon request, information about your Unemployment Compensation Claim and earnings may be provided to other state and federal agencies for income and eligibility verification.

PLEASE COMPLETE ITEMS NUMBERED 1 THROUGH 36 (PLEASE PRINT). Complete items 37 and 38 on the supplemental form for other employment you have had during the last two (2) years.

	FOR OFFICE USE ONLY. DO NOT WRITE IN THIS BOX

1. Name: (First, Middle, Last)

Social Security Number:

1a. Other Names Used During Employment

EFF DATE	M	D	Y	DATE FILED	M	D	Y

2. Local Mailing Address

Street Address: Apt. #

CLAIM STATUS	NEW	ADD'L	R/O	T	REQUALIFY		
TYPE:	UC	X	FE	CWC	EB	OTHER	

City: State: Zip: County:

ISSUE: (circle one)   UCB-13   MODS   STDK   METHOD
NO
YES — enter flag codes

3. Telephone Number: Alternate phone number:
( ) –   or ( ) –

1.
2.
3.
4.

	LOCAL OFFICE	FIPS	COUNTY	SDA
	IND	W/S	ERP	MCS

4. Date of Birth: Month   Day   Year   **5. Sex:** ☐ M ☐ F   **6. Height/ Weight**

ID VERIFIED:
TYPE: EXPIRATION DATE:

7. Ethnic Identification (statistical use only)
- ☐ White, not Hispanic (1)
- ☐ Black, not Hispanic (2)
- ☐ Hispanic (3)
- ☐ American Indian or Alaskan Native (4)
- ☐ Asian, Pacific Islander (5)

Primary DOT Code: Secondary DOT Code:

8. Circle the number which corresponds to the highest grade you completed:
1. Did not finish High School — Highest grade completed was:
   1   2   3   4   5   6   7   8   9   10   11   12
2. High School Diploma or GED
3. AA or Post Secondary Vocational/Technical Certificate of Completion
4. BS/BA   5. MS/MA   6. Doctorate

Title III EDWAA Eligibility Reason:
- ☐ 1. Terminated, laid off or notified of layoff, UC elig. or exhausted, not likely to return to occupation or industry.
- ☐ 2. Terminated, laid off or notified of layoff because of permanent closing of plant or facility
- ☐ 3. Long-term unemployed w/ limited opportunities for employment in same or similar occupation (including age barrier)
- ☐ 4. Unemployed, self-employed

9. Are you handicapped as defined in Section 504 of the Rehabilitation Act of 1973? ☐ Yes ☐ No
Definition: A person is handicapped if he or she has a physical or mental impairment which substantially limits one or more major life activities; has a record of such impairment; or is regarded as having such impairment.
NOTE: This information will be used for statistical purposes only; is requested on a voluntary basis; and will be kept confidential.

10. I am a citizen of the United States. ☐ Yes ☐ No   Alien Reg. #:
If no, I am authorized to work in this country. ☐ Yes ☐ No   Expiration Date:

10a. Citizenship: ☐ US Citizen/Nationalized ☐ Cuban Entrant   ☐ Lawfully Admitted Alien/Refugee ☐ Haitian Entrant ☐ Other   **10b.** If not fluent in English, what language do you prefer to use?

11. Most Recent Employer:

Employer's Street Address:

City   State   Zip

Employer's Local Mailing Address (if different than above):

City   State   Zip

Dates Worked:
FROM: MO.   DAY   YR   TO: MO.   DAY   YR

Total Gross Earnings with this employer: $ _____

Employer's Telephone Number: Salary Rate: $ _____ Per _____ Hr, Wk, Month, Year

Total Gross Earnings since Sunday of this week: $ _____

Occupation or Title:

Reason for Separation:
- ☐ Permanent Lay-off
- ☐ Temporary Lay-off
- ☐ Quit or Voluntary Lay-off
- ☐ Working Reduced Hours
- ☐ Suspension
- ☐ Leave of Absence
- ☐ Discharged, Job Performance
- ☐ Discharged, Other

Tools/Equipment Used:

Are you scheduled to return to work for this employer?
☐ Yes   When? _____
☐ No

Explain Reason for Separation:

12. Have you received, or will you receive any of the following payments?
Severance Pay	☐ Yes	☐ No	Amount: $ _____
Wages in Lieu of Notice	☐ Yes	☐ No	
Vacation Pay	☐ Yes	☐ No	From: _____ To: _____

LES FORM JB-310 (REV. 7/95)

13. Are you currently employed, self-employed or have you been self-employed in the past year?	☐ Yes	☐ No
14. Is there any reason you cannot seek or accept full time employment?	☐ Yes	☐ No
15. Have you refused any offer of work since you became unemployed?	☐ Yes	☐ No
16. Are you presently enrolled in school or vocational training?	☐ Yes	☐ No

17. Do you have specific plans to enroll in school or vocational training within the next 12 months? ☐ Yes ☐ No

If yes, When? _____ (date)

18. During the past 18 months, have you:
    a. Been in the Military Service? ☐ Yes ☐ No
    b. Held a Federal Civilian Job? ☐ Yes ☐ No
    c. Worked in any other state? ☐ Yes ☐ No

19. Are you receiving, or will you recive a retirement pension? ☐ Yes ☐ No

If Yes, Date Payment Began/Will Begin: _____ Employer's Name: _____

20. If you receive, or will receive payments from Workers Compensation, is it classified as:
    Temporary Total   Yes ☐   No ☐   Permanent Total   Yes ☐   No ☐
    Temporary Partial   Yes ☐   No ☐   Permanent Partial   Yes ☐   No ☐

21. Are you a veteran? ☐ Yes ☐ No   Did you separate from the service within the last 48 months? Yes ☐ No ☐

21a. If you are a veteran:		22. Are you the spouse of a 100% disabled veteran (service connected), or a veteran killed in the line of duty, an MIA, or POW?
	Most Recent	Prior Service	
Branch of Armed Service Military:			Yes ☐ No ☐
21b. Date of Entry:			
21c. Date of Release:			23. Were you on active duty for over 180 days? Yes ☐ No ☐
21d. Occupational Specialty:			
			24. Were you discharged for a service connected disability? Yes ☐ No ☐
25. Were you in a reserve unit that served on active duty during a period of war or in a campaign or expedition? Yes ☐ No ☐			if Yes, give the percent of your VA disability: ____ %

If yes, specify:
War, Campaign, or Expedition: _____   Dates Served: _____

26. Are you a member of a labor union? ☐ Yes   ☐ No
If Yes, provide Union Name and Number: _____

27. What type of transportation do you normally use to get to work? ☐ Private ☐ Public ☐ None ☐ Other

28. What active driver's licenses do you possess?
    ☐ A. Tractor Trailer over 13 Tons   ☐ D Single Vehicle Greater than 4 Tons and Less than 13 tons,
    ☐ B Single Vehicle 13 Tons or More   or more than 80 inches Wide
    ☐ C Endorsed Vehicle Less than 13 Tons   ☐ E Regular Operator's License

29. What other types of active licenses or certificates do you possess? Nursing, Teaching, etc.

30. What types of work are you seeking?	31. What is the minimum salary you are willing to accept?
	$ _____ Per: _____

In order to determine which other services may be appropriate for you, please answer the following questions:
Answering these questions is optional, but if answered, may allow us to provide more services to you.

32. Have you ever been convicted of a felony or misdemeanor? ☐ No ☐ Yes If yes, please specify: ☐ Felony
(Benefits will not be denied based on your answer)   ☐ Misdemeanor

33. How many are there in your family including yourself?	34. What is your yearly family income?	35. Are you receiving Food Stamps? ☐ Yes ☐ No

36. Are you receiving AFDC (Aid to Families with Dependent Children)? ☐ Yes ☐ No

Claimant Signature: _____   Date: _____

Interviewer Signature: _____   Date: _____

Number 8: If you did not graduate from high school, put a circle around the number of the last grade you finished. You have a choice of numbers 1–12. If you did graduate from high school or have a GED, put a circle around that choice. If you have a two-year college degree or a vocational diploma, put a circle around that choice. If you have a four-year college degree or a post graduate degree, put a circle around the appropriate choice.

Number 9: You do **not** have to answer this question. It is like Number 7. The government uses this for information only. If you want to answer it, put a (✓) in the appropriate box.

Number 10: Put a (✓) in the appropriate box(es). If you are an authorized alien, fill in your registration number and the date your registration ends.

Number 10a: Put a (✓) in the appropriate box.

Number 10b: If you do not speak English very well, write the language you speak best.

Number 11: NOTE: Be careful. There are many lines to Number 11.

First, give the name and address of your last employer. Below this, there are two extra lines to use if your last employer has a different local address. Next, give your last employer's telephone number. To the right, fill in your salary—what you were earning. Below that, put a (✓) in the box that tells why you are no longer at that job. Then, give an explanation.

To the right is a separate area. It begins with *Dates Worked*. Fill in the month, day, and year you started that job and the month, day, and year you ended that job. Below that, fill in your total gross income. Next, fill in your total gross income this week. After that, write your occupation. Below that, write the names of any tools or equipment you use for your occupation. Then, put a (✓) in the appropriate box. If you checked *yes*, fill in *when*.

NOTE: You are finished with Number 11. Go back and make sure you filled in each line correctly.

Number 12: Put a (✓) in the appropriate boxes. If you answer *yes* in any box, fill in the *amount* and *from/to*.

Numbers 13 through 20: Put (✓'s) in the *yes* or *no* boxes. If you answer *yes* to Number 17, fill in *when*. If you answer *yes* to Number 19, fill in where it says *date payment begins* and *employer's name*.

Number 21: Put (✓'s) in the boxes that say *yes* or *no*. If you are **not** a veteran, do not fill in Numbers 21a through 21d, Numbers 23, 24, or 25. If you are a veteran, give the appropriate information.

Number 22: Put a (✓) in the box that says *yes* or *no*.

Number 26: Put a (✓) in the box that says *yes* or *no*. If you check *yes*, state the union's name and number.

Number 27: Put a (✓) in the appropriate box. If you drive your own car or ride with someone else, put a (✓) in the box that says *private*. If you take a bus or train, put a (✓) in the box that says *public*.

Number 28: Put a (✓) in the appropriate box.

Number 29: Fill in other licenses or certificates you have.

Number 30: Fill in the kind of work you are looking for.

Number 31: Fill in your minimum salary.

Numbers 32 through 36: You do **not** have to answer these questions. If you decide to answer them, put (✓'s) in the appropriate boxes. If you answer *yes* in Number 32, mark *Felony* or *Misdemeanor*.

Number 33: Fill in the number of people in your family. Include yourself.

Number 34: Fill in your yearly income.

At the bottom of this form, sign your name and fill in the date.

Unit 2
Money Matters

Now that you have a job and are earning a salary, how will you manage your money? Unit 2 of this book will help you with some of the important forms you will need for careful money management.

The first thing you will need is a **checking account**. Putting your money into a bank is much safer than carrying cash. A checking account also makes it easier for you to pay your bills. There are several forms related to your checking account. First, you will use a **deposit slip** for putting money into the bank. Second, you will learn how to write a **check**. Next, you will learn how to keep your **checkbook register**—the record of your deposits and checks. Finally, you will learn how to read your **bank statement**.

Unit 2 ends with two federal income tax forms—the **1040EZ** and the

1040A. The most important thing you can learn about income tax forms is that you can fill in your own form. Although many people worry about income tax forms, all you really need to do is read carefully and do some simple addition and subtraction.

Remember the general rules for all forms. (1) Read the form all the way through first. (2) Use a pen and PRINT. (You may fill in some forms in this unit in script.) (3) After you are finished, check the form for any mistakes.

Form **1040A**	Department of the Treasury—Internal Revenue Service **U.S. Individual Income Tax Return** (O)		1994	IRS Use Only—Do not write or	OMB

Label (See page 16.)

Use the IRS label. Otherwise, please print or type.

Your first name and initial · Last name

If a joint return, spouse's first name and initial · Last name · Apt. no.

Home address (number and street). If you have a P.O. box, see page 17.

City, town or post office, state, and ZIP code. If you have a foreign address, see page 17. · Yes · No

Your socia

Spouse's s

For Pri
Paperv
Reduc
Notice

Note:
not ch
reduce

Presidential Election Campaign Fund (See page 17.)
Do you want $3 to go to this fund?
If a joint return, does your spouse want $3 to go to this fund?

Check the box for your filing status
(See page 17.)
Check only one box.

1 ☐ Single
2 ☐ Married filing joint return (even if only one had income)
3 ☐ Married filing separate return. Enter spouse's social security number above and full name here. ▶
4 ☐ Head of household (with qualifying person). (See page 18.) If the qualifyi but not your dependent, enter this child's name here. ▶
5 ☐ Qualifying widow(er) with dependent child (year spouse died ▶ 19

Figure your exemptions
(See page 20.)

If more than seven dependents, see page 23.

6a ☐ **Yourself.** If your parent (or someone else) can claim you as a dependent on his or her tax return, **do not** check box 6a. But be sure to check the box on line 18b on page 2.

b ☐ **Spouse**

c **Dependents:**

(1) Name (first, initial, and last name)	(2) Check if under age 1	(3) If age 1 or older, dependent's social security number	(4) Dependent's relationship to you	(5) No. of mon lived in you home in 199

d If your child didn't live with you but is claimed as your depend
1985 agreement, check here

17

Opening a Checking Account – A Deposit Ticket

New Words

automatic deposit   a deposit that is made for you on a regular basis

deposit   to put into, as in "to put money into your account"

deposit ticket   a form for listing amounts of money put into your account

endorse   sign your name on something to show you approve

properly   correctly

singly   one at a time

Introduction

Having a checking account makes life easier in a number of ways. First, you do not have to walk around with a lot of cash. As you know, cash can be stolen or lost.

Second, you can pay bills with checks. This is better than paying with cash because your checks are records of whom you paid, how much you paid, and when you paid. Also, you should always use checks when you pay by mail. **Never send cash in the mail.**

Third, when you have a checking account, you do not have to worry about how you are going to cash your paychecks. You can deposit your paycheck into your checking account. If you want, your employer will automatically deposit your paycheck into your checking account.

Opening a checking account is easy. Pick the bank nearest your home or job. Go in and ask to see a bank officer. The officer will ask your name, address, Social Security number, and where you work. Then, the officer will ask you how much money you want to deposit. Your first deposit opens your new checking account. Now, you will be given temporary checks. You can use them until your permanent checks come in the mail. They should arrive in two to four weeks. The bank will charge a fee for printing your checks.

Your checks will have your account number printed on them. Like your Social Security number, your account number belongs to you.

Tip: When your permanent checks come, make sure the printed account number matches the printed account number on your temporary checks. Also, make sure your printed name and address are correct. If there are any problems, go to your bank immediately and let an officer know.

Sample Deposit Ticket

GEORGE AND MARY SANCHEZ
1765 SHERIDAN DRIVE
YOUR CITY, STATE 12345

1
DATE _____ July 18 19 96

CHECKS AND OTHER ITEMS ARE RECEIVED FOR DEPOSIT SUBJECT TO THE TERMS AND CONDITIONS OF THIS BANK'S COLLECTION AGREEMENT. DEPOSITS MAY NOT BE AVAILABLE FOR IMMEDIATE WITHDRAWAL.

THE BANK OF YOUR CITY
YOUR CITY, STATE 12345

	CASH →	2			LIST SINGLY. BE SURE EACH ITEM IS PROPERLY ENDORSED.
C H E C K S		3	125	00	
		4	67	50	
		5	242	97	
		6			
	TOTAL	7	435	47	
	LESS CASH RECEIVED	8	35	00	
	TOTAL	9	400	47	

10
x *George Sanchez*
CHECKING ACCOUNT DEPOSIT TICKET

⑆123456789⑆123456789123⑈

Tip: Most people write in script when they fill in a deposit ticket. You may print or use script. However, always write your signature in script.

Study the sample deposit ticket on page 18.

Directions

Number 1: All deposit tickets have a date. The date is filled in.

Number 2: This is the *CASH* line. If you are depositing cash, write the amount here. In the sample, this line is blank because there is no cash in this deposit.

Numbers 3 through 6: These lines are for the checks you are depositing. The sample has three checks—one for $125.00, one for $67.50, and the last one for $242.97.

Number 7: This is the *Total* line. Add the amounts of all your deposits. Write the total here. In the sample, add the amounts on the three checks. The total is $435.47.

Number 8: Use this line to indicate any cash you want. In the sample, you want $35.00 in cash from the checks you deposited.

Number 9: This is your total deposit. Subtract Number 8 from Number 7.

$$\begin{array}{r} \$435.47 \\ -\ 35.00 \\ \hline \$400.47 \end{array}$$

Your net deposit is $400.47.

Number 10: Sign your deposit ticket.

Practice

There is a blank deposit ticket below for practice. Using the following information, fill in the practice deposit ticket.

Today is July 20, 1996. You are making two deposits. One is for $29.00 in cash, and the other is a check for $100.00.

Question: How much money do you have in your checking account after this deposit?

Tip: The bank will give you a copy of your deposit ticket. This is a receipt. Always keep your receipt.

Blank Deposit Ticket

		CASH →			LIST SINGLY. BE SURE EACH ITEM IS PROPERLY ENDORSED.
	C H E C K S				
		TOTAL			
		LESS CASH RECEIVED			
		TOTAL			

GEORGE AND MARY SANCHEZ
1765 SHERIDAN DRIVE
YOUR CITY, STATE 12345

DATE _____ 19 _____
CHECKS AND OTHER ITEMS ARE RECEIVED FOR DEPOSIT SUBJECT TO THE TERMS AND CONDITIONS OF THIS BANK'S COLLECTION AGREEMENT. **DEPOSITS MAY NOT BE AVAILABLE FOR IMMEDIATE WITHDRAWAL.**

THE BANK OF YOUR CITY
YOUR CITY, STATE 12345

X_____
CHECKING ACCOUNT DEPOSIT TICKET

⑆123456789⑆123456789123⑈

A Personal Check

New Words

identification   something that shows who you are

memo   a note to record something

Introduction

Now you have a checking account with $529.47 in it. You can use your checks to pay your bills. For example, when you get your electric bill, write a check for the amount on the bill. Then, mail it to your local electric company.

You can also use your checks to pay for things when you are shopping. If you want to buy something in a store, you can write a check. The salesperson will ask for some identification when you pay with a check. You can use your driver's license and a credit card for identification. (You will practice filling in a driver's license application in Unit 5 and a bank credit card application in Unit 3).

If you want more cash, that is simple too. Just write a check to yourself and cash it at your bank.

Study the sample check below. There is a blank check on page 21 for practice.

NOTE: Your name and address are printed at the top of the check.

The number printed at the upper right side of the check is the check number. Check numbers are in order. This check is number 101; the next check will be number 102.

The numbers printed at the bottom are your account number.

Tip: Most people write in script when they fill in a check. You may print or use script. However, always write your signature in script.

Directions

Number 1: All checks must have a date. The date is filled in.

Number 2: Write the name of the person or company this check is going to. This check is to *Local Drugstore*.

Number 3: Fill in the amount the check is for. This check is for $27.16.

Number 4: Write the amount in words and a fraction.

Sample Personal Check

```
┌─────────────────────────────────────────────────────────────────┐
│  GEORGE AND MARY SANCHEZ                                 101      │
│     1765 SHERIDAN DRIVE                                           │
│     YOUR CITY, STATE  12345                                      │
│  Pay to the              1      July 20  19 96                   │
│  Order of  2 Local Drugstore                    $ 3  27.16       │
│  4 Twenty seven and 16/100 ~~~~~~~~~~~~~~~~~~~~~~~~~~~  Dollars   │
│  THE BANK OF YOUR CITY                                           │
│     YOUR CITY, STATE  12345                                     │
│  Memo 5 medicine                 6  Mary Sanchez                │
│  ⑆123456789⑆123456789123⑈  101                                 │
└─────────────────────────────────────────────────────────────────┘
```

20

Number 5: The memo line gives you a chance to keep a record of how you spent your money. In the sample, the check is for *medicine*.

Number 6: A check must be signed—in script. Do not print. Make sure you sign your check because unsigned checks are no good.

Tip: Make sure you write names correctly on your checks. Do not use nicknames or abbreviations. Perhaps you know someone as "TJ" Peterson, but his real name is Thomas James Peterson. Make the check out to Thomas James Peterson, not "TJ."

Practice

Using the information below, fill in the practice check. This check is number 102.

Today is July 30, 1996. You have to pay $80.00 to Daisy Day Care. The $80.00 is for child care for your son while you are at work.

Blank Personal Check

GEORGE AND MARY SANCHEZ   **102**
1765 SHERIDAN DRIVE
YOUR CITY, STATE 12345

_____ 19_____

Pay to the Order of _____ $ [   ]

_____ *Dollars*

THE BANK OF YOUR CITY
YOUR CITY, STATE 12345

Memo _____ _____

⑈ ⅼ23456789⑈ⅼ23456789ⅼ234⑊ ⅼ02

The Checkbook Register

New Words

balance In your checkbook register, *balance* means the total amount of money you have.

charges money subtracted from your account

deposit/credit money added to or credited to your account

debit/payment money subtracted or deducted from your account

register a book of records

transaction the activity or business that occurs

Sample Checkbook Register

		RECORD ALL CHARGES OR CREDITS THAT AFFECT YOUR ACCOUNT						
NUMBER	DATE	DESCRIPTION OF TRANSACTION	PAYMENT/DEBIT (-)	√ T	FEE (IF ANY) (-)	DEPOSIT/CREDIT (+)	BALANCE $	
1	7/18		$		$	$ 400 17	400	17
2	7/20					129 00	529	47
3 101	7/20	Local Drugstore	27 16				502	31
4 102	7/30	Daisy Day Care	80 00				422	31

REMEMBER TO RECORD AUTOMATIC PAYMENTS / DEPOSITS ON DATE AUTHORIZED.

Introduction

So far you have learned how to make deposits and write checks. Now you need to learn how to keep a record of these. You keep a record so you know how much money you have. This record is kept in your checkbook register.

When you make a deposit, write it in the register. Do not forget to enter any automatic deposits. If your employer deposits your paycheck into your account every Friday, every Friday you must remember to enter this in your register.

When you write a check, enter it in the register. Do not forget to enter any automatic payments. These are automatically subtracted from your account.

Look at the sample register on page 22. Notice that a payment is a debit. This money is deducted or subtracted from your account. Notice that a deposit is a credit. This money is credited to or added to your account.

Directions

Number 1: You opened your account on July 18th with $400.47.

Number 2: Next, you deposited another $129.00 on July 20th. Now, add your two deposits together. That number is your new balance, $529.47.

NOTE: All deposits are added to your balance because you are adding money.

Number 3: This is the first check you wrote. It is check number 101 to Local Drugstore for $27.16. Subtract this amount from your balance. Now you have $502.31.

Number 4: This is the second check you wrote. It is check number 102 to Daisy Day Care for $80.00. Subtract this amount from your balance. Now you have $422.31.

NOTE: All payments are subtracted from your balance because you do not have that money any more.

Using the information below, make two entries into the register.

On August 6th, you write check 103 to the Local Telephone Company for $12.33. Then on August 9th, you decide you need cash, so you write check 104 to yourself for $50. What is your new balance? (answer $359.98)

The Bank Statement

Introduction

Every month your bank will mail you a bank statement. Your bank statement is a record of every check and every deposit for that month. Your bank statement also shows any charges subtracted from your account or interest paid to it. Along with your bank statement, you will receive your canceled checks. Canceled checks are the checks you wrote, such as numbers 101 and 102. After Local Drugstore and Daisy Day Care have cashed their checks, your bank returns your checks to you.

Save your canceled checks because they are your proof of payment. For example, if you claim child care expenses as a deduction on your income tax form, you will need the canceled checks from Daisy Child Care. Another example, you paid your bill to Local Telephone Company for $12.33, but they do not have a record of your payment. You can send them a copy of your canceled check to prove that you already paid.

Each month you must make sure your checkbook register and the bank statement have the same information. Make sure all your deposits were added to your account. Also, make sure your balance and the bank's balance are the same. If there are any problems, you can always get help from a bank officer.

Tip: After you make sure that a deposit appears on the bank statement, you can throw away that deposit ticket or receipt. Only save the receipts from deposits that have not yet appeared on your bank statement.

Every bank has it own bank statement form, but the information on all bank statements is the same. Below is a sample bank statement.

THE BANK OF YOUR CITY
YOUR CITY, STATE 12345

NAME: GEORGE AND MARY SANCHEZ   ACCOUNT: 1234567891234
ADDRESS: 1765 SHERIDAN DRIVE   DATE: 08/15/96
          YOUR CITY, STATE 12345

BEGINNING BALANCE 07/18/96: $400.47   ENDING BALANCE 08/12/96: $347.98

DEPOSITS			PAYMENTS		
DATE	AMOUNT		DATE	CHECK	AMOUNT
07/18/96	$400.47		07/24/96	101	$27.16
08/06/96	$129.50		07/22/96	*	$12.00
			07/30/96	102	$80.00
			08/08/96	103	$12.33
			08/09/96	104	$50.00

*CHECK PRINTING FEE

Note: Next to each of your checks is a date. This is the date that each check cleared, not the date you wrote on the check.

Federal Income Tax Forms 1040EZ and 1040A

Introduction

By the end of January every year, you should receive a W-2 Wage and Tax Statement form from your employer. This form shows how much money you earned for the year. It also shows how much income tax was withheld from your paycheck.

You need your W-2 form in order to fill in the federal income tax form. If you have not received your W-2 form by the middle of February, let your employer know. You have until midnight, April 15th to complete and mail the federal income tax form to the government.

This section has two federal income tax forms for practice, the 1040EZ and the 1040A. You can use these forms only if you earned less than $50,000 during the year.

The 1040EZ

You can use this form if 1) you are either single or married and are filing jointly, and 2) you have no dependents.

New Words

dependents   people you support

filing status   single, married filing together, married filing separately, etc.

interest income   money you earned on money you invested

IRS   Internal Revenue Service, the federal government agency that collects taxes

joint return   a tax form when it is used by both the husband and wife filing together

refund   money you get back

spouse   husband or wife

Directions

NOTE: This tax form is read by a machine, so make sure you put your numbers inside the boxes and do not use dollar signs ($).

Label section
If the IRS mailed the 1040EZ to you, you will have a label with your name and address printed on it. Stick the label on where it says *label here*. If you do not have a label, print your name and address here. To the right, fill in your Social Security number. If you are filing a joint return, fill in your spouse's Social Security number.

Presidential election campaign section
If you want $3.00 of your tax money to go to the presidential election campaign fund, put a (✓) in the box that says *yes,* if not, put a (✓) in the box that says *no.*

NOTE: This money does not go to any one particular presidential candidate.

Income section
Number 1: Fill in the amount shown on your W-2 form.

Number 2: Fill in the amount of interest you received from your bank or any investments you have. This amount will be on your "end of year" bank or other financial statement. If you did not earn any interest, leave Number 2 blank.

Number 3: Add the amounts in Numbers 1 and 2. Write the answer here.

Number 4: Put a (✓) in either the *yes* or *no* box indicating whether you are claimed as a dependent on someone else's tax return. If you answered *yes,* do the worksheet on the back of the 1040EZ. If you answered *no,* fill in 6,250.00.

Directions continue on page 27.

Department of the Treasury—Internal Revenue Service

Form
1040EZ

Income Tax Return for Single and
Joint Filers With No Dependents (O) **1994**

OMB No. 1545-0675

**Use the
IRS label**
(See page 12.)
Otherwise,
please print.

L A B E L   H E R E

Print your name (first, initial, last)

If a joint return, print spouse's name (first, initial, last)

Home address (number and street). If you have a P.O. box, see page 12. Apt. no.

City, town or post office, state and ZIP code. If you have a foreign address, see page 12.

Your social security number

Spouse's social security number

See instructions on back and in Form 1040EZ booklet.

**Presidential
Election
Campaign**
(See page 12.)

Note: *Checking "Yes" will not change your tax or reduce your refund.*

Do you want $3 to go to this fund? ▶

If a joint return, does your spouse want $3 to go to this fund? ▶

Yes   No

Dollars   *Cents*

Income

**Attach
Copy B of
Form(s)
W-2 here.**
Enclose, but
do not attach,
any payment
with your
return.

Note: *You
must check
Yes or No.*

1 Total wages, salaries, and tips. This
should be shown in box 1 of your
W-2 form(s). Attach your W-2 form(s).   1

2 Taxable interest income of $400 or less. If the total is
over $400, you cannot use Form 1040EZ.   2

3 Add lines 1 and 2. This is your **adjusted gross income.**
If less than $9,000, see page 15 to find out if you can
claim the earned income credit on line 7.   3

4 Can your parents (or someone else) claim you on their return?
☐ **Yes.** Do worksheet
on back; enter
amount from
line G here.
☐ **No.** If **single,** enter 6,250.00.
If **married,** enter 11,250.00.
For an explanation of these
amounts, see back of form.   4

5 Subtract line 4 from line 3. If line 4 is larger than
line 3, enter 0. This is your **taxable income.** ▶ 5

**Payments
and tax**

6 Enter your Federal income tax withheld from box 2 of
your W-2 form(s).   6

7 **Earned income credit** (see page 15). Enter type
and amount of nontaxable earned income below.

7

8 Add lines 6 and 7 (don't include nontaxable earned
income). These are your **total payments.**   8

9 **Tax.** Use the amount on **line 5** to find your tax in the
tax table on pages 28–32 of the booklet. Then, enter the
tax from the table on this line.   9

**Refund
or
amount
you
owe**

10 If line 8 is larger than line 9, subtract line 9 from line 8.
This is your **refund.**   10

11 If line 9 is larger than line 8, subtract line 8 from line 9.
This is the **amount you owe.** See page 20 for details on
how to pay and what to write on your payment.   11

**Sign
your
return**

Keep a copy
of this form
for your
records.

I have read this return. Under penalties of perjury, I declare that to the
best of my knowledge and belief, the return is true, correct, and accurately
lists all amounts and sources of income I received during the tax year.

Your signature | Spouse's signature if joint return

Date | Your occupation | Date | Spouse's occupation

For Privacy Act and Paperwork Reduction Act Notice, see page 4.   Cat. No. 11329W   Form 1040EZ (1994)

Number 5: Do the subtraction as the form tells you. Write the answer here. If line 4 is larger than line 3, fill in "0".

Payments and tax section

Number 6: Fill in the amount of federal income tax withheld. Use the amount shown on your W-2 form.

Number 7: The *earned income credit* is a special credit for certain workers. To see if you qualify for this credit, get a 1040EZ instruction book from the IRS office nearest you. Then, fill in the *earned income credit* worksheet. If you do not qualify, leave Number 7 blank.

Number 8: Do the addition as the form tells you. Write the answer here.

Number 9: The IRS publishes tax tables in the back of the tax booklets. Below is a part of a tax table for you to look at. Let us say the amount you wrote for Number 5 is $9,240. Find that amount in the tax table. You will notice the table is given in ranges—$9,200 to $9,250. Read across until you are in the column with the correct filing status. There you will find the amount of tax you owe. So, if you are single with a taxable income of $9,240, you owe $1,384 in taxes.

Enter the amount you owe for Number 9.

Refund or amount you owe section

Number 10: If Number 8 is larger than Number 9, do the subtraction as the form says. Write your answer here. This is your refund.

Number 11: If Number 9 is larger than Number 8, do the subtraction as the form says. Write your answer here. This is the amount you owe to the government.

Tip: If you are getting a refund, it will be mailed to you. You will have to wait about eight weeks for it.

Sign your return section

Sign and date your 1040EZ. Fill in your occupation. Remember to keep a copy of this form for your records.

NOTE: Do not forget to attach your W-2 form to your 1040EZ tax form. Mail them both before midnight, April 15th.

The 1040A

You can use this form 1) for any filing status, and 2) if you have dependents.

New Words

annuities fixed income from investments

dividends money made from investments

IRA Individual Retirement Account

IRA distributions money received from IRA

itemize list

pension retirement income

tax exempt free from taxes

widow a woman whose husband is dead

widower a man whose wife is dead

1994 1040EZ Tax Table—*Continued*

If Form 1040EZ, line 5, is—		And you are—		If Form 1040EZ, line 5, is—		
At least	But less than	Single	Married filing jointly	At least	But less than	S
		Your tax is—				
9,000				**12,000**		
9,000	9,050	1,354	1,354	12,000	12,050	1
9,050	9,100	1,361	1,361	12,050	12,100	1
9,100	9,150	1,369	1,369	12,100	12,150	
9,150	9,200	1,376	1,376	12,150	12,200	
9,200	9,250	1,384	1,384	12,200	12,250	
9,250	9,300	1,391	1,391	12,250	12,300	
9,300	9,350	1,399	1,399	12,300	12,350	
9,350	9,400	1,406	1,406	12,350	12,400	
9,400	9,450	1,414	1,414	12,400	12,450	
9,450	9,500	1,421	1,421	12,450	12,500	
9,500	9,550	1,429	1,429	12,500	12,550	
9,550	9,600	1,436	1,436	12,550	12,600	
9,600	9,650	1,444	1,444	12,600	12,650	
9,650	9,700	1,451	1,451	12,650	12,700	
9,700	9,750	1,459	1,459	12,700	12,750	
9,750	9,800	1,466	1,466	12,750	12,800	
9,800	9,850	1,474	1,474	12,800	12,850	
9,850	9,900	1,481	1,481	12,850	12,900	1
9,900	9,950	1,489	1,489	12,900	12,950	1
9,950	10,000	1,496	1,496	12,950	13,000	
10,000				**13,000**		
10,000	10,050	1,504	1,504	13,000	13,050	
050	10		11		13,100	

Directions

Label section

If the IRS mailed the 1040A form to you, you will have a label with your name and address printed on it. Stick the label on where it says *label here*. If you do not have a label, print your name and address here. To the right, fill in your Social Security number. If you are filing a joint return, fill in your spouse's Social Security number.

If you want $3.00 of your tax money to go to the presidential election campaign fund, put a (✓) in the box that says *yes*. If you do not, put a (✓) in the box that says *no*. This money does not go to any one presidential candidate.

Filing status section

Put a (✓) in only one of the boxes—Numbers 1, 2, 3, 4, or 5. This is your filing status. If you checked Number 3, fill in your spouse's Social Security number. If you checked Number 4 and the qualifying person is a child but not your dependent, fill in the child's name. If you checked Number 5, fill in the year your spouse died.

Figure your exemptions section

Number 6a: Put a (✓) in the box that says *yourself*. Claim yourself unless someone else claims you as a dependent.

Number 6b: If you support your spouse, put a (✓) the box that says *spouse*.

Number 6c: (1) Write the names of your dependents, first name first. (2) Put a (✓) here if they are under one year old. (3) If they are over one year old, write their Social Security numbers here. (4) Tell how these dependents are related to you (for example—*son, daughter, mother, brother-in-law*). (5) Tell how many months during the past year each dependent lived with you.

Number 6d: If you have a dependent child who does not live with you, put a (✓) here.

To the right are five boxes. If you put a (✓) for 6a, write 1 in the top box. If you put a (✓) for both 6a and 6b, write 2 in the top box. In the second box, write the number of children from 6c who lived with you. In the third box, write the number of children from 6c who did not live with you.

In the fourth box, write the number of dependents from 6c who are not children.

Number 6e: Add all these numbers, and write the total in the last box.

Figure your total income section

To fill in this section of the tax form, you need to have all your records. You will need your W-2 form, your bank statements, statements from any investments you may have, and statements from unemployment compensation and/or Social Security, if this applies.

Number 7: Fill in the amount shown on your W-2.

Numbers 8a through 13b: You can skip these if your total income is shown on your W-2—in other words—you have no interest, dividends, or other sources of income.

If you must fill in numbers 8a through 13b, here are the instructions:

Number 8a: Fill in the amount shown on your bank and/or financial statement(s) for any interest you earned. If you earned more than $400, you must fill in Schedule 1. You can get this form from the IRS.

Number 8b: If you have earned any interest which is tax-exempt, fill in the amount here. If you need more information for Number 8b, see the IRS instruction book.

Number 9: If you have any money invested in stocks or bonds, write the amount of dividends you received during the year. If you earned more than $400 in dividend income, you must fill in Schedule 1.

Number 10a: If you received money from your IRA, fill in the amount here.

Number10b: Enter the taxable amount from your IRA. If you need more information, see the IRS instruction book.

Number 11a: Enter the amount of money you received from pensions and annuities.

Directions continue on page 31.

Form

1040A

Department of the Treasury—Internal Revenue Service

U.S. Individual Income Tax Return (O) 1994

IRS Use Only—Do not write or staple in this space.

OMB No. 1545-0085

Label
(See page 16.)

Use the IRS label. Otherwise, please print or type.

L A B E L   H E R E

Your first name and initial	Last name	Your social security number
If a joint return, spouse's first name and initial	Last name	Spouse's social security number
Home address (number and street). If you have a P.O. box, see page 17.	Apt. no.	
City, town or post office, state, and ZIP code. If you have a foreign address, see page 17.		

For Privacy Act and Paperwork Reduction Act Notice, see page 4.

Presidential Election Campaign Fund (See page 17.)

Do you want $3 to go to this fund? . . . .

If a joint return, does your spouse want $3 to go to this fund?

Yes | No

Note: *Checking "Yes" will not change your tax or reduce your refund.*

Check the box for your filing status
(See page 17.)

Check only one box.

1 ☐ Single

2 ☐ Married filing joint return (even if only one had income)

3 ☐ Married filing separate return. Enter spouse's social security number above and full name here. ▶ _____

4 ☐ Head of household (with qualifying person). (See page 18.) If the qualifying person is a child but not your dependent, enter this child's name here. ▶

5 ☐ Qualifying widow(er) with dependent child (year spouse died ▶ 19 ___). (See page 19.)

Figure your exemptions
(See page 20.)

If more than seven dependents, see page 23.

6a ☐ **Yourself.** If your parent (or someone else) can claim you as a dependent on his or her tax return, **do not** check box 6a. But be sure to check the box on line 18b on page 2.

b ☐ **Spouse**

c **Dependents:** (1) Name (first, initial, and last name)	(2) Check if under age 1	(3) If age 1 or older, dependent's social security number	(4) Dependent's relationship to you	(5) No. of months lived in your home in 1994

No. of boxes checked on 6a and 6b	
No. of your children on 6c who:	
• lived with you	
• didn't live with you due to divorce or separation (see page 23)	
Dependents on 6c not entered above	
Add numbers entered on lines above	

d If your child didn't live with you but is claimed as your dependent under a pre-1985 agreement, check here . . . . ▶ ☐

e Total number of exemptions claimed.

Figure your total income

Attach Copy B of your Forms W-2 and 1099-R here.

If you didn't get a W-2, see page 25.

Enclose, but do not attach, any payment with your return.

7 Wages, salaries, tips, etc. This should be shown in box 1 of your W-2 form(s). Attach Form(s) W-2. | 7

8a **Taxable** interest income (see page 25). If over $400, attach Schedule 1. | 8a

b **Tax-exempt** interest. DO NOT include on line 8a. | 8b

9 Dividends. If over $400, attach Schedule 1. | 9

10a Total IRA distributions. | 10a | 10b Taxable amount (see page 26). | 10b

11a Total pensions and annuities. | 11a | 11b Taxable amount (see page 27). | 11b

12 Unemployment compensation (see page 30). | 12

13a Social security benefits. | 13a | 13b Taxable amount (see page 31). | 13b

14 Add lines 7 through 13b (far right column). This is your **total income.** ▶ | 14

Figure your adjusted gross income

15a Your IRA deduction (see page 34). | 15a

b Spouse's IRA deduction (see page 34). | 15b

c Add lines 15a and 15b. These are your **total adjustments.** | 15c

16 Subtract line 15c from line 14. This is your **adjusted gross income.** If less than $25,296 and a child lived with you (less than $9,000 if a child didn't live with you), see "Earned income credit" on page 44. ▶ | 16

Cat. No. 11327A

1994 Form 1040A page 1

Figure your standard deduction, exemption amount, and taxable income

17	Enter the amount from line 16.	17

18a Check if: □ **You** were 65 or older □ Blind } **Enter number of boxes checked ▶** 18a
□ **Spouse** was 65 or older □ Blind }

b If your parent (or someone else) can claim you as a dependent, check here . . . . ▶ 18b □

c If you are married filing separately and your spouse files Form 1040 and itemizes deductions, see page 38 and check here. ▶ 18c □

19 Enter the **standard deduction** shown below for your filing status. **But if you checked any box on line 18a or b,** go to page 38 to find your standard deduction. **If you checked box 18c,** enter -0-.
- Single—$3,800   • Married filing jointly or Qualifying widow(er)—$6,350
- Head of household—$5,600   • Married filing separately—$3,175   **19**

20	Subtract line 19 from line 17. If line 19 is more than line 17, enter -0-.	20
21	Multiply $2,450 by the total number of exemptions claimed on line 6e.	21
22	Subtract line 21 from line 20. If line 21 is more than line 20, enter -0-. This is your **taxable income.** ▶	22

Figure your tax, credits, and payments

If you want the IRS to figure your tax, see the instructions for line 22 on page 39.

23 Find the tax on the amount on line 22. Check if from:
□ Tax Table (pages 62–67) or   □ Form 8615 (see page 40).   **23**

24a Credit for child and dependent care expenses. Attach Schedule 2.   24a

b Credit for the elderly or the disabled. Attach Schedule 3.   24b

c Add lines 24a and 24b. These are your **total credits.**   24c

25	Subtract line 24c from line 23. If line 24c is more than line 23, enter -0-.	25
26	Advance earned income credit payments from Form W-2.	26
27	Add lines 25 and 26. This is your **total tax.** ▶	27

28a Total Federal income tax withheld. If any tax is from Form(s) 1099, check here. ▶ □   28a

b 1994 estimated tax payments and amount applied from 1993 return.   28b

c **Earned income credit.** If required, attach Schedule EIC (see page 44).   28c
Nontaxable earned income:
amount ▶ _____   and type ▶ _____

d Add lines 28a, 28b, and 28c (don't include nontaxable earned income). These are your **total payments.** ▶ 28d

Figure your refund or amount you owe

29	If line 28d is more than line 27, subtract line 27 from line 28d. This is the amount you **overpaid.**	29
30	Amount of line 29 you want **refunded to you.**	30
31	Amount of line 29 you want **applied to your 1995 estimated tax.**	31
32	If line 27 is more than line 28d, subtract line 28d from line 27. This is the **amount you owe.** For details on how to pay, including what to write on your payment, see page 52.	32
33	Estimated tax penalty (see page 52). Also, include on line 32.	33

Sign your return

Keep a copy of this return for your records.

Under penalties of perjury, I declare that I have examined this return and accompanying schedules and statements, and to the best of my knowledge and belief, they are true, correct, and accurately list all amounts and sources of income I received during the tax year. Declaration of preparer (other than the taxpayer) is based on all information of which the preparer has any knowledge.

Your signature	Date	Your occupation

Spouse's signature. If joint return, BOTH must sign.	Date	Spouse's occupation

Paid preparer's use only

Preparer's signature ▶	Date	Check if self-employed □	Preparer's social security no.
Firm's name (or yours if self-employed) and address ▶		E.I. No.	
		ZIP code	

*U.S. Government Printing Office: 1994 — 375-221   ✪ *Printed on recycled paper*   **1994 Form 1040A page 2**

Number 11b: Enter the taxable amount from your pensions and annuities. If you need more information, see the IRS instruction book.

Number 12: Enter the amount of unemployment compensation you received during the year.

Number 13a: Enter the amount of Social Security benefits you received during the year.

Number 13b: Enter the taxable amount of your Social Security benefits.

Number 14: To find your *total income* for the year, add the amounts you wrote in numbers 7 through 13b. Write the total here.

Figure your adjusted gross income section

Number 15a: If you contribute to your IRA, enter the amount you contributed this year.

Number 15b: If your spouse contributed to an IRA, enter the amount he/she contributed this year.

Number 15c: Add Number 15a and 15b together. Write the answer here.

Number 16: Subtract Number 15c from Number 14. This is your *adjusted gross income*. If you qualify for the *earned income credit*, follow the IRS instructions.

Figure your standard deduction section

Number 17: Enter the amount you put for Number 16—your *adjusted gross income*.

Number 18a: Put a (✓) in the appropriate box(es). In the big box to the right, write the number of boxes you checked. If neither box is appropriate, leave this blank. Then, enter "0" in the box to the right.

Number 18b: If you are someone's dependent, put a (✓) here.

Number 18c: If you are married filing separately, follow the IRS instructions.

Number 19: Enter your *standard deduction*. If you are single, it is $3,800. If you are married filing jointly or are a qualifying widow(er), it is $6,350.

If you are a head of household, it is $5,600, If you are married filing separately, it is $3,175. If you put a (✓) next to Number 18a or 18b, see the IRS instructions. If you put a (✓) next to 18c, enter "0".

Number 20: Subtract Number 19 from Number 17. Write the answer here. If Number 19 is more than Number 17, enter "0".

Number 21: Multiply $2,450 by the total number of exemptions—the number written in box 6e. Write the answer here.

Number 22: Subtract Number 21 from Number 20. Write the answer here. If Number 21 is more than Number 20, enter "0". This is your *taxable income*.

Figure your tax section

Number 23: This is similar to finding the tax you owe on the 1040EZ. Find the amount of tax you owe from the tax table or from form 8615. Part of the tax table appears on page 32. Form 8615 is in the IRS 1040A booklet.

Enter the amount you owe here.

Numbers 24a-c: Do these only if you are claiming credit for child and dependent care or credit for the elderly or the disabled.

Number 24a: If you are entitled to a child and dependent care credit, you must fill in Schedule 2. For more information, see the IRS instruction book. Write the amount of that credit here.

Number 24b: If you are entitled to credit for the elderly or the disabled, you must fill in Schedule 3. For more information, see the IRS instruction book. Write the amount of that credit here.

Number 24c: Add numbers 24a and b, and write your answer here.

Number 25: Subtract Number 24c from Number 23. Write the answer here. If Number 24c is more than Number 23, write "O" here.

Number 26: If you received *advance earned income credit* payments, write how much here.

Directions continue on page 32.

Number 27: Add numbers 25 and 26. Write the answer here.

Number 28a: Fill in the amount of federal income tax withheld. The amount is on your W-2 form. If any tax is from Form 1099, put a (✓) in the little box. For more information, read the IRS instruction book.

Number 28b: If you paid estimated taxes, write how much was applied from the previous year's return.

Number 28c: If you qualify for the *earned income credit*, write the amount here. Also, fill in any *nontaxable earned income*. Be sure to attach Schedule EIC to your 1040A form.

Number 28d: Add numbers 28a through c. Write your answer here.

Figure your refund or amount you owe section

Number 29: If Number 28d is more than Number 27, subtract Number 27 from Number 28d. Write your answer here. This is the amount you overpaid. You are entitled to a refund.

Number 30: Write in dollars and cents how much you want refunded to you.

Number 31: If you want all or part of your refund applied to your next year's tax, write how much here.

Number 32: If Number 27 is more than Number 28d, subtract Number 28d from Number 27. Write your answer here. This is the amount you owe to the government.

Number 33: If you owe a penalty on your estimated tax, write that amount here.

Sign and date your 1040A. Fill in your occupation. If a professional tax preparer filled in this form for you, that person will fill in the paid preparer's section.

Page 64

1994 Tax Table—Continued

If Form 1040A, line 22, is—		And you are—				If Form line 22,	
At least	But less than	Single	Married filing jointly *	Married filing separately	Head of a household	At least	l
				Your tax is—			
14,000						**17,0**	
14,000	14,050	2,104	2,104	2,104	2,104	17,000	17
14,050	14,100	2,111	2,111	2,111	2,111	17,050	17
14,100	14,150	2,119	2,119	2,119	2,119	17,100	1
14,150	14,200	2,126	2,126	2,126	2,126	17,150	
14,200	14,250	2,134	2,134	2,134	2,134	17,200	
14,250	14,300	2,141	2,141	2,141	2,141	17,250	1
14,300	14,350	2,149	2,149	2,149	2,149	17,300	17
14,350	14,400	2,156	2,156	2,156	2,156	17,350	1
14,400	14,450	2,164	2,164	2,164	2,164	17,400	
14,450	14,500	2,171	2,171	2,171	2,171	17,450	17
14,500	14,550	2,179	2,179	2,179	2,179	17,500	1
14,550	14,600	2,186	2,186	2,186	2,186	17,550	17
14,600	14,650	2,194	2,194	2,194	2,194	17,600	17,
14,650	14,700	2,201	2,201	2,201	2,201	17,650	17
14,700	14,750	2,209	2,209	2,209	2,209	17,700	17
14,750	14,800	2,216	2,216	2,216	2,216	17,750	1
14,800	14,850	2,224	2,224	2,224	2,224	17,800	17
14,850	14,900	2,231	2,231	2,231	2,231	17,850	17
14,900	14,950	2,239	2,239	2,239	2,239	17,900	17
14,950	15,000	2,246	2,246	2,246	2,246	17,950	1
15,000						**18,0**	
15,000	15,050	2,254	2,254	2,254	2,254	18,000	18
	15,10		2,26		2,261		

Unit 3
Consumer Needs

We are all consumers—buyers of products and services. Unit 3 of this book is about the applications and forms consumers use.

Perhaps you qualify for a **credit card**. You will qualify if you have been working at the same place for a while and you pay your bills on time. Many people use a credit card to pay for things. You can get a credit card from a store. This kind of credit card can be used only at that store. You can also get a credit card from a bank. This kind of credit card can be used anywhere. Unit 3 gives you a practice bank credit card application.

Buying a car is one of the most exciting and important purchases a person can make. Because cars are expensive, most people have only enough money for a down payment. They finance the rest of the cost of the car with an **automobile loan**. Unit 3 has an automobile loan application. If your loan application is approved, you will be able to buy the car you want.

Good consumers look for warranties on the products they buy. You should fill in the **product warranty card** and **registration form**. Then, send them to the manufacturer. You will find these forms in this unit.

Ordering items from a catalog is a convenient way to shop. Filling in a **catalog order form** carefully will help you get quick and accurate delivery of the items you want. The catalog order form and sample catalog page will help you understand how to fill in this form.

Do not forget the general rules for filling in applications and forms. (1) Read the form all the way through first. (2) Use a pen and PRINT. (3) After you are finished, check the form for any mistakes.

Complete, fold, moisten and seal for mailing

Barnett Bank Credit Card Application

FOR BAN

Bank #

Check One:
☐ MasterCard ☐ Visa

☐ Yes, I would like Overdraft Protection.

Barnett Checking Account Number: | | | | | (Last)

Name: (First) (M.I.)

Date of Birth: / / Social Security Number: (City) (State) (Zip)

Home Phone: ( ) (Street) (City) (State) (Zip)

Address: (Street) (City) (State) (Zip)

If P.O. Box number please also indicate street address: (Street)

Previous Address: Mortgage Holder/Landlo

☐ Own Home ☐ Other
☐ Rent ☐ Live with Parents

Monthly Rent/Mortgage Pmt.: $ Position:

Business Phone: ( )

Employer: (City) (State) (Zip)

Business Address: (Street) Position:

Previous Employer: Source:

(City) (St

*Other Sources of Income (Alimony, child support or separate maintenance income need not be disclosed if you do not wish to have it considered as a basis of repaying this obligation.) (Street)

Name and Address of Nearest Relative not living with you: BALANCE OWING

ACCOUNT NUMBER

NAME OF CREDITOR

Other Barnett Accounts: Checking, Savings, Money Market Acco. ccount Nur

Credit Card Application

New Words

alimony   money you get from your ex-spouse or money you give to your ex-spouse

applicant   a person who fills in an application

certify   guarantee, confirm

creditor   a person or company to whom you owe money

disclose   make known, reveal

interest   In this form, *interest* means money you pay for using the money you owe.

joint credit   credit given to you and someone else based on your combined ability to pay back the loan

landlord   a person or company you pay rent to

obligation   legal promise, agreement

overdraft protection   If you write a check for more money than you have in your checking account, overdraft protection will cover that check with money borrowed from your credit card. You will pay interest on this amount as you would with any charges on your credit card.

verify   prove the truth of

Abbreviations used in this form

mo.   month

wk.   week

yrs.   years

pmt.   payment

Introduction

Most people like to have credit cards. They are another way of paying for things.

Credit means that you can pay later for what you buy now. For example, if you decide to buy a new television set, you can "charge" it on your credit card. At the end of each month, your bank—or the company you got your credit card from—will mail a statement to you. The statement lists all of the purchases you made.

You can pay the amount you owe with one of your checks. If you pay your total bill immediately, you will not pay interest. Sometimes you will want to make a few smaller payments instead of one big payment. You can pay the minimum amount indicated on your credit card statement. Remember, if you decide to make small payments, you pay interest on the rest of the money you owe.

Tip: The interest rate on credit cards is very high. It is best to pay your bill every month because you avoid paying interest fees. If you must make small payments, try to pay as much as you can each month. You pay interest only on what you owe. The less you owe, the less interest you pay.

Directions

At the top of the form, put a (✓) in the box that says which credit card you want, Mastercard or Visa.

Number 1: Put a (✓) in the box that says *yes* if you want overdraft protection.

Number 2: Fill in your checking account number.

Number 3: Fill in your name, first name first.

Directions continue on page 36.

Barnett Bank Credit Card Application

Check One:

☐ MasterCard ☐ Visa

FOR BANK USE ONLY

Bank #	Office #

☐ [1] Yes, I would like Overdraft Protection. | Barnett Checking Account Number: [2]

Name: (First) [3]	(M.I.)	(Last)

Home Phone: ( ) [4]	Date of Birth: [5] / /	Social Security Number: [6]

Address: [7]	(Street)	(City)	(State)	(Zip)	Length at Present Address: [8] Yrs. Mo.

If P.O. Box number please also indicate street address: [9]	(Street)	(City)	(State)	(Zip)

Previous Address: [10]	(Street)	(City)	(State)	(Zip)	Length at Previous Address: [11] Yrs. Mo.

☐ Own Home ☐ Other [12] ☐ Rent ☐ Live with Parents	Monthly Rent/Mortgage Pmt.: $ [13]	Mortgage Holder/Landlord: [14]

Employer: [15]	Position: [16]	Length at Present Employment: [17] Yrs. Mo.

Business Address: (Street) [18]	(City)	(State)	(Zip)	Business Phone: ( ) [19]	Salary or Pension: (Gross) $ [20] Wk. Mo.

Previous Employer: [21]	Position: [22]	Length of Employment: [23] Yrs. Mo.

*Other Sources of Income (Alimony, child support or separate maintenance income need not be disclosed if you do not wish to have it considered as a basis of repaying this obligation.)	Source: [24]	Amount monthly: $ [25]

Name and Address of Nearest Relative not living with you: [26]	(Street)	(City)	(State)	(Zip)

NAME OF CREDITOR	ACCOUNT NUMBER	BALANCE OWING	MONTHLY PAYMENT AMOUNT
[27] a			
b			
c			

Other Barnett Accounts: Checking, Savings, Money Market Account/Account Numbers

1. [28] a	3. c
2. b	4. d

Co-Applicant (Complete only if joint account is desired.): [29]	Home Phone: ( ) [30]	Social Security Number: [31]

Date of Birth: [32]	Relationship To Applicant: [33]

Residence Address: [34]	(Street)	(City)	(State)	(Zip)	Length at Present Employment: [35] Yrs. Mo.

Employer: [36]	Position: [37]	Salary or Pension: (Gross) $ [38] Wk. Mo.

Employer Address: [39]	(Street)	(City)	(State)	(Zip)	Business Phone: ( ) [40]

*Other Sources of Income (Alimony, child support or separate maintenance income need not be disclosed if you do not wish to have it considered as a basis of repaying this obligation.)	Source: [41]	Amount monthly: $ [42]

NOTE: This application is submitted to obtain credit privileges and I/We (hereinafter "I" or "my") certify that all information herein is true and complete. I authorize Barnett Card Services (Barnett) to retain property of this application, to rely on the foregoing to check and verify my credit, employment and salary history, to secure follow-up credit reports concerning my creditworthiness and to exchange information about my account with proper persons, creditors, and credit bureaus. Barnett is also authorized to exchange this application, the information contained in or submitted with this application, the credit evaluation or processing hereof, and, if approved, all payment and other relationship information to Barnett Banks, Inc. or any affiliate or service corporation of Barnett Banks, Inc. without my notice or approval. I authorize my employer (present or future), bank and other references listed to release and/or verify information to Barnett at any time. I acknowledge that this application is subject to approval of credit and acceptance by Barnett at its principal office in Florida and that any credit extended pursuant hereto is extended by Barnett from its principal office in Florida. If this application is approved, I agree to abide by the terms of the Cardmember Agreement and Disclosure Statement which shall be issued by Barnett from time to time.

There are costs associated with the use of the credit card. For specific information regarding the cost, please write us at Barnett Bank, P.O. Box 2686, Jacksonville, Florida 32231-0099 or call us at 1 (800) 323-6276. This offer may expire without notice.

If OVERDRAFT PROTECTION is checked, I understand that if I have a joint Checking Account with OVERDRAFT PROTECTION, the persons listed on that account are authorized to activate the credit card's available credit line for OVERDRAFT PROTECTION coverage. If OVERDRAFT PROTECTION is approved by Barnett for my Checking Account, I agree to the provisions of the OVERDRAFT PROTECTION Agreement and coverage will not be effective until Barnett has approved OVERDRAFT PROTECTION and has sent the OVERDRAFT PROTECTION Agreement.

X_____   X_____

Signature of Applicant   Date   Signature of Co-Applicant (if joint)   Date

Number 4: Fill in your telephone number. Remember to put your area code in the parentheses ( ).

Number 5: Fill in your birth date.

Number 6: Fill in your Social Security number.

Number 7: Fill in your complete address.

Number 8: Write how long—in years and months—you have lived at this address.

Number 9: If your address is a PO box number, fill that in here.

Number 10: Fill in your previous address—where you lived before.

Number 11: Write how long—in years and months—you lived at this address.

Number 12: Put a (✓) in the appropriate box.

Number 13: Write the amount of your monthly rent or monthly mortgage payment.

Number 14: Write the name of the person or company you pay rent to or make your mortgage payments to.

Number 15: Fill in the name of your employer.

Number 16: Fill in the position or job you have.

Number 17: Write how long—in years and months—you have had this job.

Number 18: Fill in your employer's address.

Number 19: Fill in your employer's telephone number.

Number 20: Write your salary. Give either the weekly figure or the monthly figure. Do not give both.

Number 21: Give the name of your previous employer.

Number 22: Give the position or job you had.

Number 23: Write how long you had this job.

Number 24 and 25: If you have other sources of income, such as alimony or child support, write these sources here. Then, fill in the amount. If you do **not** want these other sources of income considered as part of your total income, do **not** fill in Numbers 24 and 25.

Number 26: Fill in the name and address of your nearest relative who does not live with you.

Number 27a through c: List your creditors. Fill in the name, your account number, the balance you owe, and the amount of your monthly payment.

Number 28a through d: If you have any other accounts at your bank, fill in the types of accounts and account numbers here.

Numbers 29 through 42: Do **not** fill in these numbers unless you want a joint account. If you want a joint account, the other person is the co-applicant. Have the co-applicant fill in Numbers 29 through 42.

Sign and date the application at the bottom. If you have a co-applicant, have that person sign and date the application as well.

If your application is approved, your credit card will be mailed to you in two to four weeks.

Application for an Automobile Loan

New Words

bankruptcy   the condition of being unable to pay your bills

dealer   a person or store that sells you a product

down payment   Your first payment for something—initial amount of money paid. You pay the rest of the money owed in installments.

finance   pay for something over a period of time

guarantor   a person or group who gives a promise to repay

installment   a partial payment (Monthly installments are partial payments.)

merchandise   manufactured goods, things bought and sold

mortgage   a loan taken out over a very long period of time to pay for a house or other property

repossessed   taken back because of nonpayment

union   an organized group of workers in the same trade

Abbreviations used in this form

acct.   account

est.   estimate

mtge.   mortgage

no.   number

Introduction

A car is one of the most expensive things you will ever buy. However, one of the nice things about having a good job and good credit is you do not have to pay for the car all at once. You can save enough money for a down payment and finance the rest.

You can borrow the rest of the money from a bank or directly from the credit company at the car dealer. Borrowing money to pay for a car is like using your credit card. The credit company loans you the money to pay for the car. Then, you are charged interest for the use of the money. You make monthly installment payments until you have paid back all the money you borrowed plus the interest.

When you select the car you want, the dealer will give you a loan application. The amount of money you give as a down payment will be subtracted from the price of the car. Then, you will know how much money you need to borrow. You will borrow enough to pay for the car.

Directions

NOTE: This form is similar to the credit card application. Much of the information asked for is the same. You have already completed the credit card application, so this form should be easy for you.

Applicant section

Number 1: Fill in your name, last name first.

Number 2: Fill in your age.

Number 3: Fill in your date of birth—month, day, year.

Number 4: Fill in the number of dependents you have. If none, fill in "0".

Number 5: Fill in your complete address.

Directions continue on page 39.

Ford Motor Credit Company

APPLICATION STATEMENT (Please Print)

APPLICANT

Last Name 1	First Name	Middle Initial J ☐ Jr. S ☐ Sr. 2	Age 3	Date of Birth / /	No. of Dep. 4

Present Address (Number And Street) 5 | City | State | Zip Code | County

Phone in Applicant's Home? 6 1 ☐ Yes 2 ☐ No | Phone Number Area Code 7 ( ) | 1 ☐ Own Home 2 ☐ Buying Home 8 | 3 ☐ Living with Relatives 4 ☐ Leasing/Renting | 5 ☐ Own/Buying Mobile Home | Lived There 9 Yrs. Mos. | Military Status 10 | In Reserves 11 ☐ Yes ☐ No

Name And Address Of Landlord Or Mortgage Holder 12 | Rent or Mtge. Pmt. $13 | Driver's License No. and State 14

Previous Address (Street, City, State and Zip Code) 15 | Lived There 16 Yrs. | Yrs. in Area 17 | Est. Annual Mileage 18

Level Of Education (Age Under 27 Only) 19 | 1 ☐ 4 Year College Grad. 2 ☐ 2 Year College Grad. | 3 ☐ Special Training 4 ☐ Some College | High School Grad? 5 ☐ Yes 6 ☐ No | Name of School _____ Field of Study _____ 20 | Degree Received _____ Year Graduated _____

APPLICANT'S EMPLOYMENT

Current Employer Name 21 | Address

Applicant's Occupation 22 | Time On Job 23 Yrs. Mos. | Employer's Phone Number 24 Area Code ( ) | Applicant's Gross Monthly Salary $25

Supervisor's Name 26 | Soc. Sec. No. (If Military, State Rank) 27 | Badge/Dept. No. 28 | Union Or Local No. 29

Previous Employer's Name 30 | Time On Previous Job 31 Years | Previous Employer's Address 32

* Alimony, child support or separate maintenance income need not be revealed if you do not wish to have it considered as a basis for repaying this obligation. | *Source of Other Income 33 ⟶ | *Other Monthly Income $34

APPLICANT'S CREDIT DATA

Bank References (And Branch) (Name Acct. Maintained In, If Other Than Above) 35 | 1 ☐ Savings & Checking 2 ☐ Checking Only 36 3 ☐ Savings Only 4 ☐ No Account

Creditor's Name And Address, Or Branch	Name Acct. Maintained In, If Other Than Above	Account Number	Date Opened	High Credit	No. Of Instalments And Monthly Payment Amount	Date Of Last Payment	Unpaid Balance
(Previous Cars Financed By Or Leased Through) (1)37 a					@		
(2) b					@		
(Other Credit) (3) c					@		
(4) d					@		

Name And Address Of Applicant's Nearest Relatives Not In Household (1)38 a | Phone No. | Relationship

(2) b | Phone No. | Relationship

Name And Address Of Applicant's Personal Friends Known Over One Year (1)39 a | Phone No.

(2) b | Phone No.

Have You Ever Had A Car Or Other Merchandise Repossessed? 40 ☐ No ☐ Yes If Yes, When? ⟶ Month Year / | Have You Ever Filed Bankruptcy? 41 ☐ No ☐ Yes If Yes, When? ⟶ Month Year /

Is Applicant Obligated To Make Alimony, Child Support Or Separate Maintenance Payments? 42 ☐ No ☐ Yes ⟶ If Yes, Amount To Be Paid Per Month Is $

FOR SELLER'S USE ONLY

(1) Cash Price (Incl. tax, title, reg. fees) . . . . $ _____ (1)
(2) Down Payment: Cash $ _____
    Net Trade $ _____ $ _____ (2)
    (Trade Allow. $ _____ Owed on Trade $ _____)
(3) Unpaid Balance of Cash Price (1−2) . . . . . . $ _____ (3)
(4) Other Charges
    (Specify) $ _____ , $ _____ $ _____ (4)
(5) Amount Financed (3 & 4) . . . . $ _____ (5)
(6) Finance Charge . . . . $ _____ (6)

(7) Time Balance (5 & 6) . . . . $ _____ (7)
(8) Payable In _____ Mo. Instalments of . . . . $ _____ (8)
Annual Percentage Rate _____ % Used Car Miles _____

☐ New ☐ Used | Year | Make | Model | Body Style

Vehicle Identification Number | Optional Equipment ☐ Air ☐ P/S ☐ P/B ☐ Auto Tr. Other

Trade Yr. | Make | Model | Body Style | Dealer Name

JOINT OR OTHER APPLICANT OR PARTY DATA

Do Not Complete This Section Unless: (Check Applicable Block)
☐ Application Is For Joint Credit With Another Person, Or Guarantor.
☐ Applicant Relying On Income From Alimony, Child Support, Or Separate Maintenance Or On Income Or Assets Of Another Person As The Basis For Repayment Of The Credit Requested.

Last Name | First Name | Middle Initial ☐ Jr. ☐ Sr. | Address (Street, City, State & Zip Code)

Employer (Firm Name, Address) | Age | Date of Birth / / | Phone No. | Relationship To Applicant (If Any)

Gross Monthly Salary $ | Occupation | Time on Job _____ Yrs. _____ Mos. | Employer's Phone No. Area Code ( ) | Soc. Sec. No. (If Military, State Rank)

Credit Reference(s) And Name Acct. Maintained In, If Other Than Above (1) | ‡Source of Other Income ⟶ | ‡Other Monthly Income $

(2) | Have You Ever Had A Car Or Other Merchandise Repossessed? ☐ No ☐ Yes If Yes, When? ⟶ Month Year /

(3) | Have You Ever Filed Bankruptcy? ☐ No ☐ Yes If Yes, When? ⟶ Month Year /

‡ Alimony, child support or separate maintenance income need not be revealed if you do not wish to have it considered as a basis for repaying this obligation.

- Applicant(s) Prefer Payments To Come Due On The _____ Of The Month.
- For The Purpose Of Securing Credit From You, I/We Certify That The Above Information Is True And Complete To The Best Of My/Our Knowledge. Applicant(s) Further Certify That I/We Have Attained The Age Of Majority. Applicant(s) Authorize You To Check My/Our Credit And Employment History And To Provide And/Or Obtain Information About Credit Experience With Me/Us.

Applicant Signature _____ Date _____ | Joint Applicant Signature Only If Joint Account _____ Date _____

FC 7141-S Sep 90 Previous editions may be used.

FORD CREDIT

38

Number 6: Do you have a telephone in your home? Put a (✓) in the appropriate box.

Number 7: Give your telephone number. Include the area code in parentheses.

Number 8: Put a (✓) in the appropriate box.

Number 9: Write how long you have lived there. Give your answer in years and months.

Number 10: Give your military status.

Number 11: Put a (✓) in the appropriate box.

Number 12: Give the name and address of your landlord or mortgage holder.

Number 13: Give the amount you pay monthly for rent or mortgage.

Number 14: Fill in your driver's license number and the state that issued it.

Number 15: Give your previous address.

Number 16: Write how long you lived there. Give your answer in years.

Number 17: Give the number of years you have lived in the area where you are now.

Number 18: About how many miles do you drive each year? Fill in this number here.

Numbers 19 and 20: If you are under 27 years old, put a (✓) in the appropriate box for level of education. Then, fill in the name of the last school you attended, what degree you received, what you studied, and when you graduated. If you are older than 27, you can leave these two items blank.

Applicant's Employment section
Number 21: Give the name of your employer.

Number 22: Give your occupation.

Number 23: Fill in how long you have had this job—in years and months.

Number 24: Fill in your employer's telephone number. Put the area code in parentheses.

Number 25: Give your monthly salary.

Number 26: Fill in the name of your supervisor at work.

Number 27: Fill in your Social Security number. If you are in the military, give your rank.

Number 28: If you have a badge or department number, fill that in here.

Number 29: If you are a member of a union, fill in the *Local Number* here.

Number 30: Give the name of your previous employer.

Number 31: Fill in how long you had this job—in years.

Number 32: Give your previous employer's address.

Number 33 and 34: If you have other sources of income such as alimony or child support, fill in these other sources here. Then, fill in the amount. If you do **not** want these other sources of income considered as part of your total income, you do **not** have to fill in Numbers 33 and 34.

Applicant's Credit Data section
Number 35: Give your bank name, branch, and account number.

Number 36: Put a (✓) in the box that says what kind of account you have.

Number 37a and b: Fill in the name of the company that financed your previous car(s). If that account was in another name, give that name here, to the right. Now, fill in the account number, the date you borrowed the money, and your credit limit. Next, give the number of installments and the amount of each installment. To the right, give the date of your last payment. Finally, if there is an unpaid balance, write the unpaid balance here. **NOTE:** Go back through Number 36a and b, and make sure you did this correctly.

Number 37c and d: Fill in any other credit you have, such as credit cards. Fill in as you did for Number 36a and b.

Number 38a and b: Give the name, address, and telephone number of two of your nearest relatives who do not live with you. Also, state your relationship to them.

Directions continue on page 40.

Number 39a and b: Give the name, address, and telephone number of two friends you have known for more than one year.

Number 40: Put a (✓) in the box that says *yes* or *no*. If you answered *yes*, tell when—month and year.

Number 41: Put a (✓) in the box that says *yes* or *no*. If you answered *yes*, tell when—month and year.

Number 42: Do you have to pay alimony or child support? Put a (✓) in the appropriate box.

If you answered *yes*, fill in how much you pay each month.

Do **not** fill in anything in the section *For Seller's Use Only.*

Do **not** fill in the Joint Applicant section unless you are applying for joint credit. If you are applying for joint credit, have your co-applicant fill in this section.

At the bottom, sign and date the application. If this is a joint application, have your co-applicant sign and date it as well.

Warranty Card and Registration Form

New Words

appliance equipment used in a household, such as a refrigerator, vacuum cleaner, toaster, or washer/dryer

correspondence written communication

model name or number given to all items of a certain kind by their manufacturer

rating plate place on an item, usually the back or bottom, where the model and serial number are found

serial number number given to each specific piece of merchandise

validate approve or confirm

Introduction

As a smart consumer, make sure that what you buy has a warranty. A warranty is your guarantee that what you paid for is well made and will work for a certain period of time.

When you buy things like appliances and electronic equipment, you get a warranty card and registration form to fill in and mail to the manufacturer. This registers your product and puts your warranty into effect.

Directions

NOTE: On the top left side, it says **Please Print**.

Number 1: Fill in your name, last name first. Put a (✓) for *Mr.*, *Mrs.*, or *Ms.* to show your correct title.

Numbers 2 and 3: Fill in your complete address.

Numbers 4 and 5: Fill in the name and address of the dealer who sold you the product.

Number 6: Fill in the model and serial number of the product. Then, give the date—month and year—when you bought this product.

WARRANTY CARD
Complete and mail today!

Please Print

( ) Mr.
( ) Mrs.
( ) Ms.

1 _____
Last Name   First Name   Middle Initial

Address 2 _____
No. and Street

3 _____
City   State   Zip Code

Correspondence other than Warranty Cards should be addressed to:
The Eureka Company, 1201 E. Bell, Bloomington, Illinois 61701.

PURCHASED FROM:

Dealer Name 4 _____

5 _____
No. & Street   City   State

6 _____
Model No.   Type/Serial No.   Date Purchased Mo./Yr.

COPY MODEL, TYPE AND SERIAL NUMBER FROM RATING PLATE ON APPLIANCE.

Part No. 47336   Printed in U.S.A.

Now try the registration form.

NOTE: Make sure you write in the little boxes—one letter per box.

Number 1: Put a (✓) in the appropriate box—*Mr., Mrs., Ms., Miss*. Then, fill in your first name, middle initial, and last name. On the next two lines, fill in your address.

Number 2: Fill in the date you bought this product. Below, give the model number, the type, and serial number. Below that, give the dealer's name and zip code.

Number 3: Fill in your telephone number, area code first.

Number 4: Fill in the amount you paid for this product.

Number 5: Fill in your date of birth—month, day, year.

Number 6: If you live by yourself, put a(✓) in the box that says *live alone*. If you live with other people, put a (✓) in the box that says *male* or *female* and give the age(s) of that person(s).

Number 7: Put a (✓) in the appropriate box.

Number 8: Put a (✓) in the appropriate box.

Number 9: Put a (✓) in the appropriate box. If none are appropriate, leave this blank.

Notice the box at the bottom. Put a (✓) in that box if you do **not** want the company to send you information about other products or services. If you want to get more information—be on the company's mailing list—leave this blank.

You are finished. Now your product has a warranty, and you are registered with the manufacturer as the owner.

IMPORTANT!   IMPORTANT!   IMPORTANT!

Thanks for purchasing this Eureka product. Please complete the information below and return promptly to validate your warranty.

1.   1. ❏ Mr.   2. ❏ Mrs.   3. ❏ Ms.   4. ❏ Miss   11A

First Name   Initial   Last Name
[| | | | | | | | | | |]   [|]   [| | | | | | | | | | |]

Address (Number and Street)   Apt. No.
[| | | | | | | | | | | | | | | | | | | | |]   [| | | |]

City   State   Zip
[| | | | | | | | | | | | |]   [| |]   [| | | | |]

2. Date of Purchase   3. Phone
[| |] [| |] [| |]   (| |) - | | | - | | | |
Month   Day   Year

Model #:   Type   Serial #:
[| | | | | | |]   [| | |]   [| | | | | | | | | |]

Dealer Name   Zip
[| | | | | | | | | | | | |]   [| | | | |]

4. Purchase Price $ [| | |].00   5. Date of Your Birth   [| |] [| |] [| |]
   (Excluding tax)   Month   Day   Year

6. Excluding yourself, what are the ages of the other people (in years) in your household?
   ❏ Live alone
   Male Female Age   Male Female Age   Male Female Age

   ❏   ❏   [| |]   ❏   ❏   [| |]   ❏   ❏   [| |]

   ❏   ❏   [| |]   ❏   ❏   [| |]   ❏   ❏   [| |]

7. Which group best describes your family annual income?
   1. ❏ Under $15,000   4. ❏ $50,000 - $74,999
   2. ❏ $15,000 - $24,999   5. ❏ $75,000 - $99,999
   3. ❏ $25,000 - $49,999   6. ❏ OVER $100,000

8. Education: (Please check which applies)
   1. ❏ Some High School   3. ❏ College/University
   2. ❏ Completed High School 4. ❏ Graduate School

9. In the last six (6) months have you or your spouse:
   1. ❏ Purchased clothes through the mail   3. ❏ Worked in your outdoor garden
   2. ❏ Purchased gifts through the mail   4. ❏ Traveled on a vacation

Thanks for filling out this questionnaire. Your answers are important to us. Please check here if you would prefer not to obtain information on new and interesting opportunities. ❏

Part No. 47336

Catalog Order Form

New Words

C.O.D.   collect on delivery, payment due when package is delivered

expiration date   date something ends

shipping   cost of sending/mailing something

Abbreviations used in this form

qty.   quantity

ea.   each

Introduction

Everyone likes to shop, and using catalogs to do so has become very popular. This is called shopping by mail, since you do not actually go to the store to purchase your merchandise. You buy from your home using a catalog order form.

There are many reasons for shopping through the mail. You may not have the time to go to a store. Perhaps you live too far from a particular store to go there. Maybe you have been ill, and you cannot get out to shop. Some companies do not have a store for you to go to. They only have a catalog.

Ordering from a catalog is very easy. After you get your catalog, either in the mail or from

the store itself, look through it and decide what you want. Next, fill in the order form and send it along with your check to the store or company. You can also use your credit card to pay for your purchase. Then, the merchandise you ordered will be delivered to you.

Directions

After studying the pictures of the computers from this catalog company, you decide that you want the LC550. Now, you have to fill in the order form.

Number 1: Fill in the catalog page number for this computer. You will notice a small box which says this computer is shown on page 7.

Number 2: Fill in the product name. In this case, it is LC550.

Number 3: Fill in how many you want. Fill in "1."

Number 4: Fill in the cost of the LC550. It is $899.

Number 5: Fill in the total. Since you ordered only one LC550, your total is $899.

Try this: What would your total be if you ordered "2" LC550's? (answer $1,798)

Number 6: Fill in the total for the merchandise you ordered. In this case, it is $899.

Try this: What would your total be if you ordered "1" LC550 and "1" Powerbook? (answer $1,898)

Number 7: Now add $3.00 for shipping to your total of $899.

Number 8: **Do this only if you are ordering C.O.D.** For this example, you are **not** ordering C.O.D.

NOTE: If you do order something C.O.D., you must pay cash when it is delivered.

Number 9: Fill in the grand total. Add the amount you have for Number 6 and the amount for Number 7. Your grand total is $902.

Try this: What would your grand total be if you ordered "1" LC550 and "1" Powerbook? (answer $1,901)

Number 10: Fill in your daytime telephone number. Remember, include your area code.

Number 11: Write your name and complete address.

Number 12: If you want your computer delivered someplace different than the address you gave in Number 11, fill in the delivery address here.

Number 13: Put a (✓) in the appropriate box. If you are paying with your check or with a money order, you are finished with the form. Just attach your check or money order to the order form and mail it to the company. If you are paying with a credit card, you must write your credit card number in the boxes below. Then, fill in the expiration date of your credit card. Finally, sign your name.

You should have your new computer in about a week.

Unit 4
Government Applications and Forms

Many of the most important things we do have us begin by filling in government applications and forms. Driving a car, voting, and traveling to another country are controlled by either the state or federal government.

Unit 4 starts with a **driver's license** application and **parent consent** form for drivers under the age of 18. Next, you will practice a **voter registration** form. These government forms are controlled by each state. Although each state has its own applications or forms for a driver's license, parent consent, and voter registration, the information that every state asks for is almost the same. The three forms used as examples will give you an idea of what these forms are like.

Unit 4 also has a **passport application**. If you are a U.S. citizen, you must get a passport from the U.S. government if you plan to travel to another country. When you return from your trip, you will fill in a **customs declaration** form. These last two forms are controlled by the federal government. No matter what state you live in, these forms will always be the same.

As always, remember the general rules for filling in forms. (1) Read the form all the way through first. (2) Use a pen and PRINT. (3) After you are finished, check the form for any mistakes.

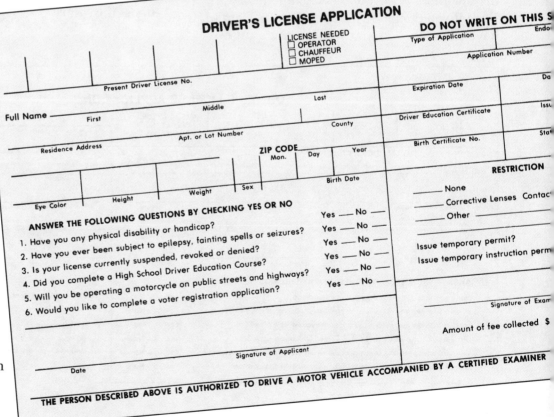

Driver's License Application

New Words

chauffeur   someone who drives a vehicle for someone else

disability   physical weakness

moped   two-wheeled vehicle

revoked   taken away; canceled

seizure   In this form, *seizure* means a sudden attack caused by a disease.

Introduction

You must have a driver's license to drive. If you drive without one, you are breaking the law. Even if you do not own a car, it is important to have a license. You may want to rent a car or borrow a friend's car someday. A driver's license is also a useful form of identification.

To get a driver's license, go to the motor vehicle bureau near you and fill in an application. You will have to take a written test. You can get a book from the motor vehicle bureau to study for the written test. After you pass the written test, you will be given an appointment for a road test. The purpose of the road test is to see if you can drive a car safely.

Once you have your license, you have a responsibility to be a safe driver at all times.

NOTE: Remember, the driver's license application in your state may look different from this sample, but the information asked for will be almost the same.

DRIVER'S LICENSE APPLICATION

LICENSE NEEDED	DO NOT WRITE ON THIS SIDE

1   ☐ OPERATOR ☐ CHAUFFEUR ☐ MOPED

Type of Application	Endorsement

Present Driver License No.

Application Number

Full Name 2 _____

First   Middle   Last

Expiration Date	Date Issued

3

Residence Address   Apt. or Lot Number   County

Driver Education Certificate	Issuing School

4   ZIP CODE

Mon.	Day	Year

Birth Certificate No.	State & County

5

Eye Color   Height   Weight   Sex   Birth Date

RESTRICTION

_____ None

6   **ANSWER THE FOLLOWING QUESTIONS BY CHECKING YES OR NO**

1. Have you any physical disability or handicap?   Yes ___ No ___
2. Have you ever been subject to epilepsy, fainting spells or seizures?   Yes ___ No ___
3. Is your license currently suspended, revoked or denied?   Yes ___ No ___
4. Did you complete a High School Driver Education Course?   Yes ___ No ___
5. Will you be operating a motorcycle on public streets and highways?   Yes ___ No ___
6. Would you like to complete a voter registration application?   Yes ___ No ___

_____ Corrective Lenses   Contact Lens ___

_____ Other _____

Issue temporary permit?   Yes ___ No ___

Issue temporary instruction permit?   Yes ___ No ___

Signature of Examiner

7 _____

Date   Signature of Applicant

Amount of fee collected $ _____

THE PERSON DESCRIBED ABOVE IS AUTHORIZED TO DRIVE A MOTOR VEHICLE ACCOMPANIED BY A CERTIFIED EXAMINER

Directions

Number 1: If you move to a different state, you will need to change your license. Fill in the number of your current license here. Next, put a (✓) in the appropriate box. If you want to drive a car, check *operator*.

Number 2: Fill in your name, first name first.

Numbers 3 and 4: Fill in your address.

Number 5: Write your eye color—blue, brown, green, or hazel. Then, fill in your height in feet and inches. Next, give your weight in pounds. Fill in "M" or "F" for sex, and finally give your date of birth—month, day, year.

Number 6: Put a (✓) next to *yes* or *no* for each of the six questions.

Number 7: Write the date, and sign your name.

NOTE: Do **not** write on the right side of this form.

Good luck with your road test.

Parent Consent for Driver Application of Minor Under 18

New Words

consent   approve, agree

custody   legal care, protection

guardian   a person who has legal custody of you

notarized   certified

witnessed   watched by an official

Introduction

Some states will allow minors—people under the age of 18—to get a driver's license. If you are a minor, you will need your parent's or guardian's consent before you can get a license. If you are the parent or guardian of a minor child, you will have to give your consent.

NOTE: Remember, the parent consent form in your state may look different from this sample, but the information asked for is almost the same.

Directions

Number 1: If you are the minor, fill in your name. If you are the parent or guardian, fill in the minor's name.

Number 2: If you are the minor, fill in your date of birth. If you are the parent or guardian, fill in the minor's date of birth.

Numbers 3 and 4: **NOTE:** Only one parent or guardian needs to sign here. The signature must be notarized, or the form needs to be signed in front of the driver's license examiner. Either parent or guardian signs, and the notary or examiner fills in the rest.

Number 5: The minor's employer signs here.

NOTE: If you are the minor, you must show your birth certificate to the examiner. If you are married, you do not have to show your birth certificate.

HSMV 71022   (REV. 1/87)S   STATE OF FLORIDA
Department of Highway Safety and Motor Vehicles   DIVISION OF DRIVER LICENSES
Parent Consent For Driver Application of Minor Under 18

We (or I) do hereby consent that [1] _____ ,
                                            FIRST   MIDDLE   LAST
Date of Birth [2] _____ , a minor, be granted a Florida Driver License and do hereby assume the obligations,
imposed by Florida Law, Section 322.09, unless and until we (or I) notify the Department to withdraw this consent.

[3] _____   [4] _____   [5] _____
    FATHER'S OR GUARDIAN'S SIGNATURE   MOTHER'S SIGNATURE   EMPLOYER'S SIGNATURE

State of Florida: State of Florida: State of Florida:
County of _____   County of _____   County of _____
Sworn and subscribed to before me this ____   Sworn and subscribed to before me this ____   Sworn and subscribed to before me this ____
_____ day of _____ 19 ____   _____ day of _____ 19 ____   _____ day of _____ 19 ____

AFFIX   Notary Public or   AFFIX   Notary Public or   AFFIX   Notary Public or
SEALS   D.L. Examiner   SEALS   D.L. Examiner   SEALS   D.L. Examiner

My commission expires: _____   My commission expires: _____   My commission expires: _____

   INSTRUCTIONS: 1. This form must be signed by one parent having custody.
                        2. All signatures must be notarized, or witnessed by examiner.
                        3. This form and birth certificate must be presented to examining office by all applicants under 18 unless married.
                        4. Signing this form constitutes consent for the minor to also obtain an operator license between the ages of 16 and 18, unless you notify the Department to withdraw this consent.

Voter Registration

New Words

optional   left to your choice

party affiliation   association with a political party, such as Democrat or Republican

register   sign up for something, enroll

suffix   In this form, *suffix* means something added at the end of your name, such as *Jr.* for junior.

Introduction

As a U.S. citizen, you have the right to vote. When there is an election, you have the chance to say who should run the government. If you do not vote, you give up the right to help run your government. Voting is a privilege of all citizens.

Voting is also your way of saying how you want your tax money spent. Remember, you pay income tax which is deducted from your paycheck.

Before you can vote, you must register. Call the Board of Elections near you to find out where to get a voter registration form. In many states, you can register to vote and get your driver's license at the same time.

NOTE: Remember, the voter registration form in your state may look different from this sample, but the information asked for is almost the same.

Directions

Number 1: Put a (✓) in the appropriate box. Remember, you can **not** vote if you are not a U.S. citizen.

Directions continue on page 52.

1	Are you a U. S. citizen? ☐ Yes ☐ No If NO, you cannot register to vote.	**Official Use Only**
2	Check boxes that apply: ☐ New Registration ☐ Address Change ☐ Party Change ☐ Name Change	

3	Last Name	Suffix (circle) Jr. Sr. II III IV	First Name	Middle Name/Initial	**4** Sex (circle) M F

5	Address Where You Live (legal residence)/do not give P.O. Box	Apt./Lot/Unit	City/Town/Village	Zip Code

6	Address Where You Get Your Mail (if different from # 5)	Zip Code	**7** County Where You Live (legal residence)

8	Date of Birth (month/day/year)	**9** Race/Ethnicity - (see instructions)	**10** Social Security No. (optional)	**11** Daytime Phone No. (optional)

12	Party Affiliation -- check one box only (see instructions) ☐ Democratic Party ☐ Other Party (write name below) _____ ☐ Republican Party ☐ None	**16** **Oath:** I do solemnly swear (or affirm) that: • I will protect and defend the Constitution of the United States and the Constitution of the State of Florida. • I am qualified to register as an elector under the Constitution and laws of the State of Florida. • I am a U. S. citizen. • I am a legal resident of Florida. • All information on this form is true. I understand that if it is not true, I can be convicted of a felony of the third degree and fined up to $5,000 and/or imprisoned for up to five years. SIGNATURE - Sign or mark on line in box below.
13	Former Name If Making A Name Change	
14	Name and Address Where You Were Last Registered. Name _____ Address _____ City County State Zip Code	_____ Date_____
15	Do You Need Assistance to Vote? ☐ Yes ☐ No	

Number 2: Put a (✓) in the appropriate box(es). **NOTE:** If you are changing your name, address, or party affiliation, you can use this form.

Number 3: Fill in your last name. To the right, circle any suffix you use. If you do not use a suffix, do not circle anything. Next, fill in your first name, then your middle name or initial.

Number 4: Circle *M* or *F.*

Number 5: Write your address.

Number 6: If you get your mail at a different address, write that here.

Number 7: Write the name of the county where you live.

Number 8: Give your date of birth—month, day, year.

Number 9: Below is a copy of the race/ethnicity choices from the voter registration form. Write the number of the race/ethnic group that best describes you.

Race/Ethnicity (Box 9):

Enter the number that best describes you:

(1) American Indian or Alaskan Native
(2) Asian or Pacific Islander
(3) Black, not of Hispanic origin
(4) Hispanic
(5) White, not of Hispanic origin

Number 10: **This is optional.** Fill in your Social Security number.

Number 11: **This is optional.** Fill in your daytime telephone number.

Number 12: Put a (✓) in the appropriate box. If you do not want to be associated with any party, put a (✓) in the box that says *None.*

Number 13: **Do this only if you are changing your name.** Write your previous name.

Number 14: **Do this only if you were registered before.** Write your name and address as it appeared on your previous registration.

Number 15: Put a (✓) in the appropriate box.

Number 16: Sign this form. Enter the date at the bottom.

A voter registration identification card will be mailed to you.

Passport Application

New Words

depart   leave

identical   same in every way

issued   given

mandatory   required

naturalize   grant citizenship

submit   give, hand in

Introduction

After you have been working for a while, you will get a paid vacation. Maybe you will want to spend your vacation in a place outside the United States.

If you travel out of the United States, you must have a passport. Without a passport, you cannot come back into the United States.

To get a U.S. passport, go to a post office, passport office, or county courthouse near you. These places have passport applications. Bring your birth certificate and some other form of identification. If you are a naturalized citizen, bring your naturalization papers. You will also have to bring two photographs of yourself. Have professional passport pictures taken. They will be the right size and format. Finally, be prepared to pay the application fee. You can pay with one of your checks.

Your passport will be good for ten years.

Directions

Number 1: Fill in your name, first name first. Use the second line for your last name.

Number 2: Fill in your mailing address—where you want your passport mailed. You have three lines for this.

Number 3: Write "M" for male or "F" for female.

Number 4: Fill in your place of birth.

Number 5: Fill in your date of birth—month, day, year.

Number 6: Fill in your Social Security number. You must give your Social Security number. If you do not have a Social Security number, fill in "0's" and Passport Services will report this to the IRS.

Number 7: Fill in your height—feet and inches.

Directions continue on page 55.

UNITED STATES DEPARTMENT OF STATE

APPLICATION FOR ☐ PASSPORT ☐ REGISTRATION
SEE INSTRUCTIONS—TYPE OR PRINT IN INK IN WHITE AREAS

1. NAME FIRST NAME   MIDDLE NAME

LAST NAME

2. MAILING ADDRESS

STREET

CITY, STATE,
ZIP CODE

COUNTRY   IN CARE OF

☐ 5 Yr. ☐ 10 Yr.   Issue
                    Date _____
R   D   O   DP
End. # _____   Exp. _____

3. SEX   **4. PLACE OF BIRTH** City, State or Province, Country   **5. DATE OF BIRTH**   **6. SEE FEDERAL TAX** SOCIAL SECURITY NUMBER
☐   LAW NOTICE ON
Male Female   Mo. Day Year   REVERSE SIDE

7. HEIGHT   **8. COLOR OF HAIR**   **9. COLOR OF EYES**   **10. (Area Code) HOME PHONE**   **11. (Area Code) BUSINESS PHONE**

Feet Inches   **12. PERMANENT ADDRESS** (Street, City, State, ZIP Code)   **13. OCCUPATION**

14. FATHER'S NAME   BIRTHPLACE   BIRTH DATE   U.S. CITIZEN   **16. TRAVEL PLANS** (Not Mandatory)
                                                         ☐ YES ☐ NO   COUNTRIES   DEPARTURE DATE

15. MOTHER'S MAIDEN NAME BIRTHPLACE   BIRTH DATE   U.S. CITIZEN
                                                         ☐ YES ☐ NO   LENGTH OF STAY

17. HAVE YOU EVER BEEN ISSUED A U.S. PASSPORT?   YES ☐   NO ☐   IF YES, SUBMIT PASSPORT IF AVAILABLE.   ☐ Submitted
IF UNABLE TO SUBMIT MOST RECENT PASSPORT, STATE ITS DISPOSITION: COMPLETE NEXT LINE
NAME IN WHICH ISSUED   PASSPORT NUMBER   ISSUE DATE (Mo., Day, Yr.)   DISPOSITION

SUBMIT TWO RECENT
IDENTICAL PHOTOS

FROM 1" TO 1-3/8"

2" × 2"

18. HAVE YOU EVER BEEN MARRIED? ☐ YES   ☐ NO   DATE OF MOST RECENT MARRIAGE   Mo. Day Year

WIDOWED/DIVORCED?   ☐ YES   ☐ NO   IF YES, GIVE DATE   Mo. Day Year

SPOUSE'S FULL BIRTH NAME   SPOUSE'S BIRTHPLACE

19. IN CASE OF EMERGENCY, NOTIFY (Person Not Traveling With You)   RELATIONSHIP
(Not Mandatory)
FULL NAME

ADDRESS   (Area Code) PHONE NUMBER

20. TO BE COMPLETED BY AN APPLICANT WHO BECAME A CITIZEN THROUGH NATURALIZATION
I IMMIGRATED TO THE U.S.   I RESIDED CONTINUOUSLY IN THE U.S.   DATE NATURALIZED (Mo., Day, Yr.)
(Month, Year)   From (Mo., Yr.)   To (Mo., Yr.)
                                                                 PLACE

21. DO NOT SIGN APPLICATION UNTIL REQUESTED TO DO SO BY PERSON ADMINISTERING OATH
I have not, since acquiring United States citizenship, performed any of the acts listed under "Acts or Conditions" on the reverse of this application form (unless explanatory statement is attached). I solemnly swear (or affirm) that the statements made on this application are true and the photograph attached is a true likeness of me.

Subscribed and sworn to (affirmed) before me   (SEAL)   X

Month Day Year

_____   ☐ Clerk of Court or   _____
           ☐ PASSPORT Agent   (Sign in presence of person authorized to accept application)
           ☐ Postal Employee
(Signature of person authorized to accept application)   ☐ (Vice) Consul USA At _____

22. APPLICANT'S IDENTIFYING DOCUMENTS ☐ PASSPORT ☐ DRIVER'S ☐ OTHER (Specify)   No.
                                                          LICENSE
ISSUE DATE   EXPIRATION DATE   PLACE OF ISSUE   ISSUED IN THE NAME OF

Month Day Year   Month Day Year

23. FOR ISSUING OFFICE USE ONLY (Applicant's evidence of citizenship)

☐ Birth Cert.   SR   CR   City   Filed/Issued: APPLICATION APPROVAL
☐ Passport   Bearer's Name:
☐ Report of Birth   _____
☐ Naturalization/Citizenship Cert.   No.:   Examiner Name
☐ Other:
☐ Seen &   Office, Date
   Returned   24.
☐ Attached   FEE _____ EXEC. _____ POST _____

FORM DSP-11 (12–87)   (SEE INSTRUCTIONS ON REVERSE)   Form Approved OMB No. 1405-0004 (Exp. 8/1/89)

Number 8: Fill in the color of your hair—brown, black, red, blonde, or gray.

Number 9: Fill in the color of your eyes—brown, green, blue, or hazel.

Number 10: Fill in your home telephone number, area code first.

Number 11: Fill in your telephone number at work, area code first.

Number 12: Write your permanent address.

Number 13: Fill in your occupation.

Number 14: Write your father's name, his place of birth, and date of birth. Then, put a (✓) in the appropriate box.

Number 15: Write your mother's maiden name, her place of birth, and date of birth. Then, put a (✓) in the appropriate box.

Number 16: **This is not mandatory.** If you wish, write your travel plans—where you are going, when you are leaving, and how long you will stay.

Number 17: Put a (✓) in the appropriate box. If you check *yes*, submit that passport. If you no longer have that passport, fill in your name as it appeared on that passport, the passport number, the date it was issued, and tell what happened to it (for example—lost, stolen, or expired).

Number 18: Put a (✓) in the appropriate boxes. If you check *yes*, give the date of your most recent marriage, or give the date you were widowed or divorced. Also, give your spouse's name and birthplace.

Number 19: **This is not mandatory.** Write the name and address of someone who is not traveling with you who can be contacted in case of emergency. Give that person's relationship to you and his or her telephone number.

Number 20: **Fill in only if you are a naturalized citizen.** Fill in the date you immigrated to the U.S., the dates you lived in the U.S., the date you were naturalized, and the place you were naturalized.

STOP! Do not fill in anything after this. You will be asked to sign this form in front of the person who gave you the application. That person will witness your signature.

Your passport will be mailed to you in four to six weeks.

Have a good vacation.

Customs Declaration

New Words

abroad out of the country

acquired something you bought or
were given

currency cash

declaration formal statement

equivalent equal in value

import bring into the country

monetary having to do with money

reside live

seizure taking something by force

smuggle import illegally

Introduction

When you return to the United States after
your vacation, you will have to fill in a customs declaration. Everybody, even visitors,
coming into the United States must fill in a
customs declaration.

A customs declaration is the government's way of keeping track of how much
money comes into and goes out of the
country. You can bring in or take out as
much money as you like, but if the amount
is over $10,000, you must fill in
another form.

The customs declaration is also the way
the government keeps track of how much
duty or tax you owe. If you are a U.S. resi-
dent, you can bring up to $400 worth of
merchandise into the country, duty free.
Anything you bring in with you that is
worth over $400, you will pay a tax on. If
you have to pay, you can do so with a check
or credit card.

The government also keeps track of the
plants, food, and animals coming into the

WELCOME TO THE UNITED STATES

DEPARTMENT OF THE TREASURY
UNITED STATES CUSTOMS SERVICE

FORM APPROVED
OMB NO. 1515-0041

CUSTOMS DECLARATION

19 CFR 122.27, 148.12, 148.13, 148.110, 148.111

Each arriving traveler or head of family must provide the following information (only **ONE** written declaration per family is required):

1. Name: ....
   Last   _First_   _Middle Initial_

2. Date of Birth: ..../......../........ 3. Airline/Flight ....
   Day _Month_ _Year_

4. Number of family members traveling with you...................................

5. U.S. Address: ....

   City: .... State: ....

6. I am a U.S. Citizen   YES   NO
   If No,   ☐   ☐
   Country: ....

7. I reside permanently in the U.S.   YES   NO
   If No,   ☐   ☐
   Expected Length of Stay: ....

8. The purpose of my trip is or was ☐ BUSINESS ☐ PLEASURE

9. I am/we are bringing fruits, plants, meats, food,   YES   NO
   soil, birds, snails, other live animals, farm   ☐   ☐
   products, or I/we have been on a farm or ranch
   outside the U.S.

10. I am/we are carrying currency or monetary   YES   NO
    instruments over $10,000 U.S. or foreign   ☐   ☐
    equivalent.

11. The total value of all goods I/we purchased or
    acquired abroad and am/are bringing to the U.S.
    is (see instructions under Merchandise on reverse
    side): $ ....
                                                US Dollars

▶ **MOST MAJOR CREDIT CARDS ACCEPTED.**

SIGN ON REVERSE SIDE AFTER YOU READ WARNING.

(Do not write below this line.)

INSPECTOR'S NAME	STAMP AREA
BADGE NO.	

Paperwork Reduction Act Notice: The Paperwork Reduction Act of 1980 says we must tell you why we are collecting this
information, how we will use it and whether you have to give it to us. We ask for this information to carry out the Customs,
Agriculture, and Currency laws of the United States. We need it to ensure that travelers are complying with these laws and
to allow us to figure and collect the right amount of duties and taxes. Your response is mandatory.

Statement required by 5 CFR 1320.21: The estimated average burden associated with this collection of information is
3 minutes per respondent or recordkeeper depending on individual circumstances. Comments concerning the accuracy of
this burden estimate and suggestions for reducing this burden should be directed to U.S. Customs Service, Paperwork
Management Branch, Washington, DC 20229, and to the Office of Management and Budget, Paperwork Reduction Project
(1515-0041), Washington, DC 20503.

Customs Form 6059B (092089)

country. For health reasons, certain plants, food, and animals cannot be brought into the U.S.

After you complete your customs declaration, your passport and luggage will be inspected by a customs agent.

Directions

Number 1: Fill in your name, last name first.

Number 2: Fill in your date of birth.

Number 3: Fill in your airline and flight number.

Number 4: Fill in the number of family members traveling with you.

Number 5: Give your address in the U.S. If you are a visitor, give the address of where you will be staying.

Number 6: Put a (✓) in the appropriate box. If you check *no*, tell what country you are a citizen of.

Number 7: Put a (✓) in the appropriate box. If you check *no*, tell how long you plan to stay in the U.S.

Number 8: Was your trip for business or pleasure (vacation)? Put a (✓) in the appropriate box.

Number 9: Put a (✓) in the appropriate box.

Number 10: Put a (✓) in the appropriate box.

Number 11: If you are a U.S. citizen, give the total dollar value of everything you are bringing into the U.S. If you are a visitor, give the total dollar value of gifts and business items only.

On the back of the declaration is space for you to list merchandise if what you declared in Number 11 is worth more than $1,400. The back of the declaration is shown on this page.

Now sign and date the declaration.

Welcome to the United States.

WARNING

The smuggling or unlawful importation of controlled substances regardless of amount is a violation of U.S. law.

Accuracy of your declaration may be verified through questioning and physical search.

AGRICULTURAL PRODUCTS

To prevent the entry of dangerous agricultural pests the following are restricted: Fruits, vegetables, plants, plant products, soil, meats, meat products, birds, snails, and other live animals or animal products. Failure to declare all such items to a Customs/Agriculture Officer can result in fines or other penalties.

CURRENCY AND MONETARY INSTRUMENTS

The transportation of currency or monetary instruments, regardless of amount, is legal; however, if you take out of or bring into (or are about to take out of or bring into) the United States more than $10,000 (U.S. or foreign equivalent, or a combination of the two) in coin, currency, travelers checks or bearer instruments such as money orders, checks, stocks or bonds, you are required by law to file a report on a Form 4790 with the U.S. Customs Service. If you have someone else carry the currency or instruments for you, you must also file the report. FAILURE TO FILE THE REQUIRED REPORT OR FALSE STATEMENTS ON THE REPORT MAY LEAD TO SEIZURE OF THE CURRENCY OR INSTRUMENTS AND TO CIVIL PENALTIES AND/OR CRIMINAL PROSECUTION.

MERCHANDISE

In Item 11, **U.S. residents** must declare the total value of ALL articles acquired abroad (whether new or used, whether dutiable or not, and whether obtained by purchase, as a gift, or otherwise), including those purchases made in DUTY FREE stores in the U.S. or abroad, which are in their or their family's possession at the time of arrival. **Visitors** must declare in Item 11 the total value of all gifts and commercial items, including samples they are bringing with them.

The amount of duty to be paid will be determined by a Customs officer. U.S. residents are normally entitled to a duty free exemption of $400 on those items accompanying them; non-residents are normally entitled to an exemption of $100. Both residents and non-residents will normally be required to pay a flat 10% rate of duty on the first $1,000 above their exemptions.

If the value of goods declared in Item 11 EXCEEDS $1,400 PER PERSON, then list ALL articles below and show price paid *in U.S. dollars* or, for gifts, fair retail value. If additional space is needed, continue on another Customs Form 6059B.

DESCRIPTION OF ARTICLES	PRICE	CUSTOMS USE
TOTAL		

IF YOU HAVE ANY QUESTIONS ABOUT WHAT MUST BE REPORTED OR DECLARED ASK A CUSTOMS OFFICER.

I have read the above statements and have made a truthful declaration.

SIGNATURE   DATE (Day/Month/Year)

✿U.S.G.P.O. 1990-744-875   Customs Form 6059B (092089) (Back)

Unit 5
Personal Concerns

Unit 5 of this book is about applications and forms that concern your personal life.

If you want to get married, you will need a **marriage license pre-application** or **application**. This unit has a pre-application form for you to practice with. After you are married, the state will send your license to you.

Next, you will practice with a **rental/credit application**. You will have to fill in this kind of form if you want to rent an apartment or house.

When you move to a different apartment or house, the Postal Service will send your mail to your new address if you fill in a **change of address order** form. The Postal Service will also provide you with **Postal Service postcards**. You can send these to people you know to tell them your new address.

Unit 5 will also give you practice with another Postal Service form, the **authorization to hold mail form**. If you go away on business or for vacation, you can have the post office stop delivering your mail for up to 30 days.

If you get sick and have to go to a doctor, you will have to fill in a **health history** form. This form helps your doctor know what illnesses or conditions you had in the past so you can receive proper medical treatment now.

Remember the general rules for filling in all forms. (1) Read the form all the way through first. (2) Use a pen and PRINT. (3) After you are finished, check the form for any mistakes.

RENTAL/CREDIT APPLICATION

PERSONAL INFORMATION

Interviewed By _____

Date _____   Telephone _____

Name of Applicant _____

Social Sec. No. _____   Driver's License No. _____

Present Address _____

City, State, Zip Code _____

Prior Address _____

City, State, Zip Code _____

How long have you lived at present address? _____   How long have you lived at prior address? _____

Name of Landlord _____   Telephone _____

Prior Landlord _____   Telephone _____

How many in your family? Adults ___ Children ___ Pets ___

Birth Date _____   Position _____

Employer _____   Telephone _____

How long? _____

SPOUSE INFORMATION

Name _____   Birth Date _____

Driver's License No. _____

59

Marriage License Pre-Application

New Words

annulled   canceled; made void

certified copy   legal or guaranteed copy

residence   place where you live

surname   your last name

Introduction

If you are not already married, you may want to get married someday. Perhaps you are engaged and are beginning to make wedding plans.

You are not legally married without a marriage license. It does not make a difference whether you get married in a church, temple, or courthouse. You still need to fill in a pre-application or application for a license.

In order to get a license, go to the Marriage License Bureau in your local court house or civic center and fill in a pre-application or application for a marriage license. After the wedding ceremony, the state will send you a certified copy of your marriage license.

NOTE: Each state has its own marriage pre-application or application. The sample in this unit may not look exactly like the one from your state, but the information asked for will be similar.

	MARRIAGE LICENSE PRE-APPLICATION	
	THE FOLLOWING IS REQUIRED TO PROCESS YOUR MARRIAGE LICENSE	

Application #:

GROOM'S NAME First Middle Last	DATE OF BIRTH Month / Day / Year
1	2
RESIDENCE City County State	BIRTH PLACE (State or Foreign Country)
3	4

BRIDE'S NAME First Middle Last	Maiden Surname If Different	DATE OF BIRTH Month / Day / Year
5	6	7

RESIDENCE City County State	BIRTH PLACE (State or Foreign Country)
8	9

THE INFORMATION BELOW WILL NOT APPEAR ON CERTIFICATION ISSUED BY VITAL STATISTICS, EXCEPT UPON REQUEST

FUTURE ADDRESS (Street, City, State, Zip Code)	PHONE (Area Code - Number)
10	

	Race: ☐Black ☐White ☐Other	# of this Marriage	How Last Marriage Ended:	Date Last Marriage Ended Month / Day / Year
GROOM	11		☐ Divorce ☐Death ☐Annulled	
BRIDE	Race: ☐Black ☐White ☐Other 12	# of this Marriage	How Last Marriage Ended: ☐ Divorce ☐Death ☐Annulled	Date Last Marriage Ended Month / Day / Year

13 ◆◆ DO YOU WISH TO BE MARRIED IN THIS OFFICE TODAY?   ☐YES   ☐NO

MARRIAGE APPLICATION FEE: $88.50   CEREMONY FEE: $20.00

LICENSE MUST BE RETURNED **NOT LATER THAN 10 DAYS** AFTER THE MARRIAGE CEREMONY FOR THE OFFICIAL RECORDING OF THE LICENSE WITH THE COUNTY AND THE STATE OF FLORIDA. IN ORDER TO RECEIVE A CERTIFIED COPY OF YOUR MARRIAGE LICENSE, A **SELF ADDRESSED AND STAMPED ENVELOPE** MUST BE SUBMITTED AT THE TIME OF THE APPLICATION.

CLK/CT 490 Rev. 7/94

Directions

NOTE: Do not fill in anything where it says *Application #*. The clerk at the Marriage License Bureau will fill this in.

Number 1: Fill in the groom or man's name, first name first.

Number 2: Fill in his date of birth.

Number 3: Fill in his address or residence.

Number 4: Fill in his place of birth. If he was born in the U.S., just give the name of the state. If he was born in another country, give the name of that country.

Number 5: Fill in the bride or woman's name.

Number 6: Give her maiden surname if it is different from the last name given in Number 5. If it is not different, leave Number 6 blank.

Number 7: Fill in her date of birth.

Number 8: Fill in her address or residence.

Number 9: Fill in her place of birth. If she was born in the U.S., just give the name of the state. If she was born in another country, give the name of that country.

NOTE: The information you give for Numbers 10 through 12 will **not** appear on your marriage license unless you want it to. If you want this information on your license, you must ask that it be included.

Number 10: Give your future address—where you will live after you get married. Also, give your future telephone number. Make sure you put the area code in parentheses.

Number 11: The groom should put a (✓) in the appropriate box. Then, he should write the number of this marriage. If this is his first marriage, he should write "1." If he was married once before, he should write "2." If this is not his first marriage, he should put a (✓) in the box that says *how last marriage ended*. To the right, he should give the date his last marriage ended.

Number 12: The bride should put a (✓) in the appropriate box. Then, she should write the number of this marriage. If this is her first marriage, she should write "1." If she was married once before, she should write "2." If this is not her first marriage, she should put a (✓) in the box that says *how last marriage ended*. To the right, she should give the date her last marriage ended.

Number 13: Put a (✓) in the appropriate box.

Congratulations on your marriage.

Rental/Credit Application

New Words

commencement date   beginning date

disclosure   a statement that reveals or exposes something

eviction notice   a form telling you to leave because you have not paid your rent

investigate   look into to find the truth

prior   earlier; former

tenant   a person who rents an apartment, house, or office

vacate   give up; leave

Introduction

You can buy an apartment or house. This means you are the owner of your residence. You can also rent an apartment or house. Renting means you do not own your residence. Instead, you sign a rental or lease agreement. This agreement allows you to live in the apartment or house for a period of time. You promise to pay rent and keep the place in good condition.

First, you must fill in a rental/credit application. Not all applications look like the sample here, but most ask for similar information. They usually ask where you work, whether or not you have a bank account, and where you lived before. The landlord may investigate the statements you make on the application. The landlord wants to know if you will be a good tenant and if you will pay your rent on time.

Directions

Personal Information section
Number 1: Fill in the date.

Number 2: Leave this blank. The person who interviews you will fill this in.

NOTE: Not all rental applications require an interview, but some do.

Number 3: Fill in your name.

Number 4: Fill in your telephone number.

Number 5: Fill in your Social Security number.

Number 6: Fill in your driver's license number.

Numbers 7 and 8: Write your address.

Numbers 9 and 10: Write your prior address.

Number 11: Fill in how long you have lived at your present address.

Number 12: Fill in how long you lived at your prior address.

Number 13: Write the name of your landlord.

Number 14: Write your landlord's telephone number.

Number 15: Write the name of your prior landlord.

Number 16: Fill in your prior landlord's telephone number.

Number 17: Fill in your date of birth.

Number 18: Write the number of adults, children, and pets in your family.

Number 19: Write the name of your employer.

Number 20: Fill in your position or job.

Number 21: Fill in how long you have worked at this job.

Number 22: Write your work telephone number.

Spouse Information section
NOTE: If you do not have a spouse, leave this section blank.

Directions continue on page 65.

RENTAL/CREDIT APPLICATION

PERSONAL INFORMATION

Date 1 _____ Interviewed By 2 _____

Name of Applicant 3 _____ Telephone 4 _____

Social Sec. No. 5 _____ Driver's License No. 6 _____

Present Address 7 _____

City, State, Zip Code 8 _____

Prior Address 9 _____

City, State, Zip Code 10 _____

How long have you lived at present address? 11 _____ How long have you lived at prior address? 12 _____

Name of Landlord 13 _____ Telephone 14 _____

Prior Landlord 15 _____ Telephone 16 _____

Birth Date 17 _____ How many in your family? Adults 18 _____ Children _____ Pets_____

Employer 19 _____ Position 20 _____

How long? 21 _____ Telephone 22 _____

SPOUSE INFORMATION

Name 23 _____ Birth Date _____

Social Security No. 24 _____ Driver's License No. _____

Employer 25 _____ Position _____

How long? 26 _____ Telephone _____

BANK INFORMATION

Bank Name 27 _____ Telephone _____

Address 28 _____

Checking Account No. 29 _____ Savings Account No. _____

ADDITIONAL PERSONAL REFERENCES

NAME	RELATIONSHIP	TELEPHONE
30		
31		
32		

OTHER INFORMATION

Number of vehicles (including company cars) 33 _____

Make/Model 34 _____ Year_____ Color _____ Tag No. _____ State ____

Make/Model 35 _____ Year_____ Color _____ Tag No. _____ State ____

Make/Model 36 _____ Year_____ Color _____ Tag No. _____ State ____

HAVE YOU EVER

   37   a   Filed for bankruptcy   ❑ Yes ❑ No   If yes, when?_____

       b   Been served an eviction notice or been asked to vacate a property you were renting?   ❑ Yes ❑ No

       c   Willfully or intentionally refused to pay rent when due?   ❑ Yes ❑ No   If yes, when?_____

How were you referred to us?   38

❑ Newspaper (name) _____ ❑ Realtor (name) _____ ❑ Other _____

Rental Unit applied for 39 _____

Commencement date 40 _____ Term _____ Rent/Month _____

DISCLOSURE

I/We, the undersigned, understand that _____ is the leasing agent and representative for the owner/landlord and that the leasing agent's fees will be paid by the owner/landlord. The undersigned acknowledge that this written notice was received prior to the undersigned receiving a lease agreement.

RADON GAS–Notice to Prospective Tenant: Radon is a naturally occurring radioactive gas that, when it has accumulated in a building in sufficient quantities, may present health risks to persons who are exposed to it over time. Levels of radon that exceed federal and state guidelines have been found in buildings in this state. Additional information regarding radon and radon testing may be obtained from your county public health unit.

I/We declare the foregoing information is true and correct, and I/We hereby authorize you to conduct an employment and credit check and to verify our references.

_____   _____
Applicant's Signature   Date   Co-Applicant's Signature   Date

FOR OFFICE USE ONLY – DO NOT WRITE BELOW

Application Verification	Person Contacted	Remarks
❑ Present Landlord		
❑ Previous Landlord		
❑ Applicant's Employment		
❑ Co-Applicant's Employment		
❑ Bank		
❑ Reference (1)		
❑ Reference (2)		
❑ Reference (3)		
❑ Other		
❑ Driver's License/ID ❑ Credit Bureau		

Verification completed by _____

Date_____

Remarks_____

_____

_____

_____

Monies Received		
Date	Description	Amount
	Applicant Fee	
	Deposit	

THIS APPLICATION

❑ Approved   ❑ Not Approved

Number 23: Fill in your spouse's name. Then, fill in your spouse's date of birth.

Number 24: Fill in your spouse's Social Security number. Then, fill in your spouse's driver's license number.

Number 25: Write the name of your spouse's employer. Then, fill in your spouse's position or job.

Number 26: Fill in how long your spouse has had this job. Then, write your spouse's telephone number at work.

Bank Information section
Number 27: Write the name of your bank. Then, fill in the telephone number.

Number 28: Fill in the address of your bank.

Number 29: Fill in your checking account number. Then, fill in your savings account number.

Additional Personal References section
Numbers 30 through 32: Give the names of three people who know you and will say good things about you. Then, give their relationship to you (for example—friend, sister, employer). To the right, give the telephone number for each one.

Number 33: Fill in the number of vehicles you have.

Numbers 34 through 36: Give the make/model for each vehicle (for example—Ford/Taurus). To the right, fill in the year of the vehicle. Then, fill in the color. Next, fill in the tag or license number. Finally, write the name of the state where the vehicle is registered.

Number 37a through c: Put (✓'s) in the boxes that say *yes* or *no*. If you put a (✓) next to *yes* for "a" or "c," tell *when*.

Number 38: How did you find out about this rental? Put a (✓) in the appropriate box. If it was from a newspaper ad, fill in the name of the newspaper. If it was from a realtor, fill in the name of the realtor. If it was some other way, fill in that information.

Number 39: Fill in which rental unit you are applying for. **NOTE:** Realtors have many units, so be specific. If you are applying for a house, give the exact address. If you are applying for an apartment, give the address and exact unit number (for example—407C).

Number 40: Fill in the date you want to begin your rental. Then, fill in for how long you want to rent. To the right, fill in the amount of rent per month you will pay.

Disclosure section
Sign and date your application. If you have a co-applicant, have that person sign and date the application as well.

Good luck with your move.

Change of Address Order Form

New Words

forward   In this form, *forward* means
  send onward.

discontinue   end; stop

temporary   for a limited time; not lasting

Abbreviations used in this form

RR/HCR   Rural Route/Highway Contract Route

St.   Street

Ave.   Avenue

Rd.   Road

Ct.   Court

apt.   apartment

Introduction

Now you are ready to move. You want to be
sure your mail will be delivered to your
new address.

   Go to your local post office and get a
Change of Address Order form. After you fill in
this form and return it to the post office, your
mail will be forwarded to your new address.
The Postal Service will forward your mail for
one year.

Directions

Tip: This form is a postcard. If you do not fill it
in at the post office, you can mail it in. The
postage is pre-paid. You do not have to pay for
a stamp.

**Change of
Address
Order Form**

Side A

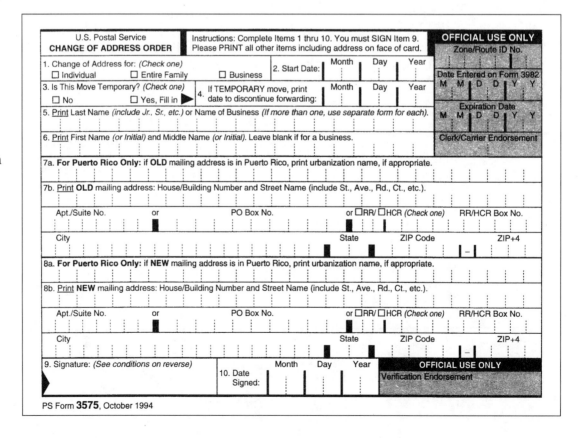

Side A

Number 1: Put a (✓) in the appropriate box.

Number 2: Give the date you want the Postal Service to start forwarding your mail.

Number 3: Put a (✓) in the box that says *yes* or *no*. If you put a (✓) in the *yes* box, fill in Number 4.

Number 4: Give the date you want to discontinue forwarding.

Number 5: Fill in your last name or the name of your business.

Number 6: Fill in your first name.

Number 7a: **NOTE:** Fill in only if your old address is in Puerto Rico. Give the urbanization name.

Number 7b: There are three lines for Number 7b. Fill in your old address. Put the information in the appropriate spaces. **NOTE:** Zip + 4 is the long version of your Zip code (for example— 33173-1224). Fill in your complete Zip code. If you know only the first five numbers, fill those in.

Number 8a: **NOTE:** Fill in only if your new address is in Puerto Rico. Give the urbanization name.

Number 8b: There are three lines for Number 8b. Fill in your new address. Put the information in the appropriate spaces.

Number 9: Sign here.

Number 10: Fill in the date.

Side B
Fill in the city, state, and Zip code of your old post office. There is a line for this at the bottom. Then, mail this form to your old post office. Your old post office will make sure your mail is forwarded.

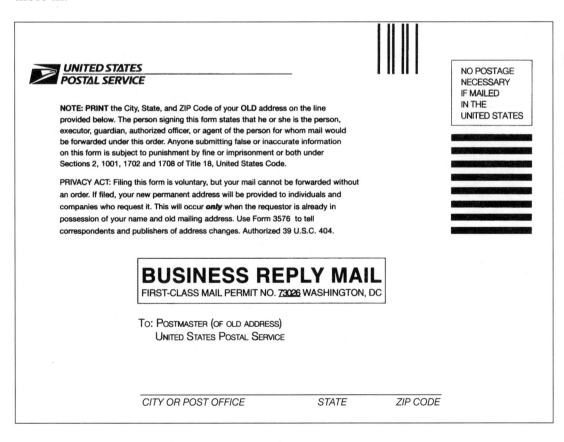

Change of Address Order Form

Side B

Postal Service Postcard

Introduction

You have notified the post office to forward your mail. But, you can do something to help get your mail to your new address. You can let people know you have moved. By notifying your friends, family, and business associates, you will not have to wait for your mail to be forwarded. Your mail will come directly to your new address.

Directions

NOTE: This form is a postcard too. However, you must put a stamp on this one.

Tip: The Postal Service will give you as many of these postcards as you need. Ask for Form 3576.

Side A
Number 1: Fill in the date you want people to start sending mail to your new address.

Postal Service Postcard

Side A

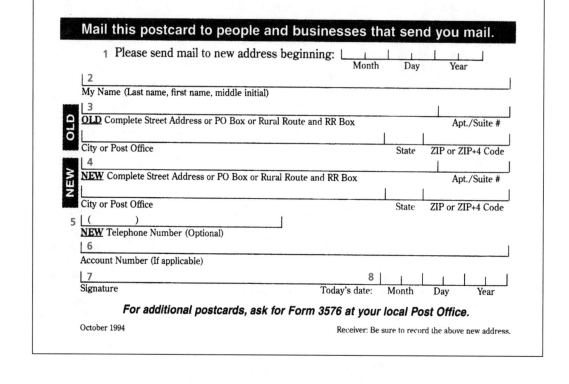

Number 2: Fill in your name, last name first.

Number 3: **NOTE:** There are two lines for Number 3. Fill in your *old* address. Make sure you include all the information.

Number 4: **NOTE:** There are two lines for Number 4. Fill in your *new* address. Make sure you include all the information.

Number 5: This is optional. Write your *new* telephone number.

Number 6: If you have an account with the Postal Service, write that number here. If you do not have an account, leave this blank.

Number 7: Sign here.

Number 8: Fill in the date.

Side B

Number 1: Fill in the name of the person you are sending this postcard to.

Number 2: If you are sending this postcard to a business, write the name of that business here.

Number 3: **NOTE:** There are two lines for Number 3. Fill in the complete address of the person or business you are sending this postcard to.

Remember, put a stamp on the postcard before you mail it.

▶ **SPEED MAIL DIRECTLY TO YOUR NEW ADDRESS**
MAIL THIS POSTCARD TO FRIENDS, FAMILY MEMBERS, BUSINESSES, AND PUBLISHERS TO INFORM THEM OF YOUR MOVE

Place
Stamp
Here

1 _____
Name
2 _____
If Applicable, Name of Business
3 _____
Complete Street Address or PO Box or Rural Route and RR Box   Apt./Suite #

_____
City or Post Office   State   ZIP or ZIP+4 Code

Postal Service Postcard

Side B

Authorization to Hold Mail

New Words

accumulated gathered into a heap or large mass

authorization the act of giving permission

resume begin again

Introduction

Perhaps you have to leave home for more than a few days. Maybe you are going on a vacation for two weeks. Maybe you have to travel on business. If there will be no one at your home to get your mail, what do you do?

You can go to the post office and fill in an Authorization to Hold Mail form so your mail will not be delivered to your house or apartment. Instead, your mail will accumulate at the post office. If you let mail accumulate at your home, you let burglars know you are not there. It is safer to let the Postal Service keep your mail until you return. The Postal Service will hold your mail for up to 30 days.

Authorization to Hold Mail
UNITED STATES POSTAL SERVICE

This service has a 30 - day limit. See DMM 153.19.

Postmaster - Please hold mail for:

Name(s)
1

Address
2

Begin Holding Mail (Date)	Resume Delivery (Date)
3	4

A. I will pick up all accumulated mail when I return and understand that mail delivery will not resume until I do. (This is suggested if your return date may change or if no one will be at home to receive mail.)
5 ☐

B. Please deliver all accumulated mail and resume normal delivery on the ending date shown above.
6 ☐

Customer Signature
7

For Post Office Use Only

Date Received

Clerk	Bin Number
Carrier	Route Number

Customer Option A Only

Carrier: Accumulated mail has been picked up. Resume delivery on:
8 _____   By: _____

PS Form **8076**, August 1990   GPO : 1991 0 - 292-992

Directions

Number 1: Fill in your name.

Number 2: Fill in your complete address.

Number 3: Write the date you want the Postal Service to start holding your mail.

Number 4: Write the date you want the Postal Service to resume delivery of your mail.

NOTE: Fill in either Number 5 or Number 6. Do **not** fill in both.

Number 5: Put a (✓) in this box if you will pick up your mail when you get home. The Postal Service will not resume delivery until you pick up your accumulated mail.

Number 6: Put a (✓) in this box if you want the Postal Service to resume normal delivery on the date you wrote in Number 4.

Number 7: Sign here.

Number 8: **NOTE:** Fill this in only if you had put a (✓) in the box for Number 5. When you return to the post office to pick up your accumulated mail, write the date you want delivery resumed. Then sign your name.

Health History Form

New Words

allergies negative physical reactions to substances such as animals or dust

complications unexpected problems or difficulties

conditions In this form, *conditions* are diseased or abnormal parts of the body.

confidential secret; private

currently now; at the present time

examination In this form, *examination* means being carefully looked at by a doctor.

hazardous substances dangerous materials

hospitalization the act of being hospitalized; being placed in a hospital

medications medicine that heals or cures

omissions things left out or not included

pharmacy a drugstore; a place where medicines and drugs are sold

provider a person or thing that gives, supplies, or makes something available

symptom a sign of something

Introduction

No one likes to think about getting sick or being hospitalized, but it happens. People get sick or injured and need medical care.

If you get sick or injured, you will either go to a group health care provider or an individual doctor. If this is your first visit, you will be asked to fill in a health history form. This form lets your health care provider or doctor know about your past illnesses and conditions. It is very important to fill in this form correctly. Your medical treatment now and in the future may depend on the information you give in your health history.

If you have group medical insurance, your doctor or health care provider will ask you for the name of your insurance company and your policy number. Your claim will be filed electronically. In most cases, your insurance will pay for much of your medical care.

Directions

Number 1: Fill in your name.

Number 2: Fill in the date.

Number 3: Write your age.

Number 4: Write your date of birth.

Number 5: Fill in the date of your last physical examination.

Number 6: Fill in the reason you are visiting your health care provider or doctor.

Symptoms section
Put a (✓) in the box(es) next to any symptom(s) you have or have had in the past year. If you are a woman, remember to fill in the information asked for in the last five lines.

Conditions section
Put a (✓) in the box(es) next to any condition(s) you have or have had in the past.

Medications section
List the names of any medications you are taking now. Give the name and telephone number of the pharmacy that filled the prescription(s).

Allergies section
Fill in the names of any medications or substances you are allergic to.

Directions continue on page 75.

HEALTH HISTORY
(Confidential)

Name 1 _____ Today's Date 2 _____

Age 3 _____ Birthdate 4 _____ Date of last physical examination 5 _____

What is your reason for visit? 6 _____

SYMPTOMS Check (✓) symptoms you currently have or have had in the past year.

GENERAL
- ☐ Chills
- ☐ Depression
- ☐ Dizziness
- ☐ Fainting
- ☐ Fever
- ☐ Forgetfulness
- ☐ Headache
- ☐ Loss of sleep
- ☐ Loss of weight
- ☐ Nervousness
- ☐ Numbness
- ☐ Sweats

MUSCLE/JOINT/BONE
Pain, weakness, numbness in:
- ☐ Arms
- ☐ Back
- ☐ Feet
- ☐ Hands
- ☐ Hips
- ☐ Legs
- ☐ Neck
- ☐ Shoulders

GENITO-URINARY
- ☐ Blood in urine
- ☐ Frequent urination
- ☐ Lack of bladder control
- ☐ Painful urination

GASTROINTESTINAL
- ☐ Appetite poor
- ☐ Bloating
- ☐ Bowel changes
- ☐ Constipation
- ☐ Diarrhea
- ☐ Excessive hunger
- ☐ Excessive thirst
- ☐ Gas
- ☐ Hemorrhoids
- ☐ Indigestion
- ☐ Nausea
- ☐ Rectal bleeding
- ☐ Stomach pain
- ☐ Vomiting
- ☐ Vomiting blood

CARDIOVASCULAR
- ☐ Chest pain
- ☐ High blood pressure
- ☐ Irregular heart beat
- ☐ Low blood pressure
- ☐ Poor circulation
- ☐ Rapid heart beat
- ☐ Swelling of ankles
- ☐ Varicose veins

EYE, EAR, NOSE, THROAT
- ☐ Bleeding gums
- ☐ Blurred vision
- ☐ Crossed eyes
- ☐ Difficulty swallowing
- ☐ Double vision
- ☐ Earache
- ☐ Ear discharge
- ☐ Hay fever
- ☐ Hoarseness
- ☐ Loss of hearing
- ☐ Nosebleeds
- ☐ Persistent cough
- ☐ Ringing in ears
- ☐ Sinus problems
- ☐ Vision – Flashes
- ☐ Vision – Halos

SKIN
- ☐ Bruise easily
- ☐ Hives
- ☐ Itching
- ☐ Change in moles
- ☐ Rash
- ☐ Scars
- ☐ Sore that won't heal

MEN only
- ☐ Breast lump
- ☐ Erection difficulties
- ☐ Lump in testicles
- ☐ Penis discharge
- ☐ Sore on penis
- ☐ Other

WOMEN only
- ☐ Abnormal Pap Smear
- ☐ Bleeding between periods
- ☐ Breast lump
- ☐ Extreme menstrual pain
- ☐ Hot flashes
- ☐ Nipple discharge
- ☐ Painful intercourse
- ☐ Vaginal discharge
- ☐ Other

Date of last menstrual period_____

Date of last Pap Smear_____

Have you had a mammogram?_____

Are you pregnant?_____

Number of children_____

CONDITIONS Check (✓) conditions you have or have had in the past.

- ☐ AIDS
- ☐ Alcoholism
- ☐ Anemia
- ☐ Anorexia
- ☐ Appendicitis
- ☐ Arthritis
- ☐ Asthma
- ☐ Bleeding Disorders
- ☐ Breast Lump
- ☐ Bronchitis
- ☐ Bulimia
- ☐ Cancer
- ☐ Cataracts

- ☐ Chemical Dependency
- ☐ Chicken Pox
- ☐ Diabetes
- ☐ Emphysema
- ☐ Epilepsy
- ☐ Glaucoma
- ☐ Goiter
- ☐ Gonorrhea
- ☐ Gout
- ☐ Heart Disease
- ☐ Hepatitis
- ☐ Hernia
- ☐ Herpes

- ☐ High Cholesterol
- ☐ HIV Positive
- ☐ Kidney Disease
- ☐ Liver Disease
- ☐ Measles
- ☐ Migraine Headaches
- ☐ Miscarriage
- ☐ Mononeucleosis
- ☐ Multiple Sclerosis
- ☐ Mumps
- ☐ Pacemaker
- ☐ Pneumonia
- ☐ Polio

- ☐ Prostate Problem
- ☐ Psychiatric Care
- ☐ Rheumatic Fever
- ☐ Scarlet Fever
- ☐ Stroke
- ☐ Suicide Attempt
- ☐ Thyroid Problems
- ☐ Tonsillitis
- ☐ Tuberculosis
- ☐ Typhoid Fever
- ☐ Ulcers
- ☐ Vaginal Infections
- ☐ Venereal Disease

MEDICATIONS List medications you are currently taking

ALLERGIES To medications or substances

Pharmacy Name_____ Phone_____

FAMILY HISTORY Fill in health information about your family.

Relation	Age	State of Health	Age at Death	Cause of Death	Check (✓) if, your blood relatives had any of the following: Disease	Relationship to you
Father					Arthritis, Gout	
Mother					Asthma, Hay Fever	
Brothers					Cancer	
					Chemical Dependency	
					Diabetes	
					Heart Disease, Strokes	
Sisters					High Blood Pressure	
					Kidney Disease	
					Tuberculosis	
					Other	

HOSPITALIZATIONS

Year	Hospital	Reason for Hospitalization and Outcome

Have you ever had a blood transfusion? ☐ Yes ☐ No
If yes, please give approximate dates. _____

SERIOUS ILLNESS/INJURIES	DATE	OUTCOME

PREGNANCY HISTORY

Year of Birth	Sex of Birth	Complications if any

HEALTH HABITS Check (✓) which substances you use and describe how much you use.

Caffeine	
Tobacco	
Drugs	
Other	

OCCUPATIONAL CONCERNS
Check (✓) if your work exposes you to the following:

Stress	
Hazardous Substances	
Heavy Lifting	
Other	
Your occupation:	

I certify that the above information is correct to the best of my knowledge. I will not hold my doctor or any members of his/her staff responsible for any errors or omissions that I may have made in the completion of this form.

_____   _____
Signature   Date

_____   _____
Reviewed By   Date

#21758 – Medical Arts Press 1-800-328-2179

Family History section

Give the following information about your father, mother, brothers, and sisters: their age, state of health, age when they died, and what caused their death. Then, put a (✓) next to the name of any disease(s) your blood relatives have. Next, write the relative's relationship to you (for example—aunt, brother, father).

Hospitalizations section

Fill in the following information for any hospitalizations: the year you were hospitalized, the name of the hospital, and the reason for being hospitalized. Also, write the outcome (for example—released from hospital after surgery). At the bottom of this section, put a (✓) in the box that says *yes* or *no*. If you put a (✓) in the *yes* box, give the dates.

Serious Illness/Injuries section

Fill in any serious illness or injury you have had. Give the date of the illness or injury. Then, write the outcome (for example—broken leg healed).

Pregnancy History section

This section is for women only. How many children do you have? Fill in the year each child was born. Then, fill in the sex of that child. Finally, write any complications you had during that pregnancy.

Health Habits section

Put a (✓) next to any substance(s) you use and tell how much you use that substance(s).

Occupational Concerns section

Put a (✓) next to anything listed that you are exposed to at work. Then, fill in your occupation.

At the bottom, sign and date this form.

Hope you are feeling better soon.